Let's Talk Dog Business Strategy

The Dog Trainer's Guide to Ideal Clients, More Money and Freedom

**Jo Moorcroft &
Vicky Davies**

Let's Talk Dog Business Strategy: The Dog Trainers Guide to Ideal Clients, More Money and Freedom

©2024 Rebel Core Collective T/A Canine Business Academy

All rights reserved. No part of this book may be reproduced, stored in a retrieval system or transmitted in any form or by any means (electronic, mechanical, photocopy, recording, scanning or other) except for brief quotations in critical reviews or articles, without the prior written permission of the publisher.

ISBN: 9781068791703 Paperback

Published by: Inspired By Publishing

The strategies in this book are presented primarily for enjoyment and educational purposes. Every effort has been made to trace copyright holders and obtain their permission for the use of copyright material.

The information and resources provided in this book are based upon the authors' personal experiences. Any outcome, income statements or other results, are based on the authors' experiences and there is no guarantee that your experience will be the same. There is an inherent risk in any business enterprise or activity and there is no guarantee that you will have similar results as the author as a result of reading this book.

The author reserves the right to make changes and assumes no responsibility or liability whatsoever on behalf of any purchaser or reader of these materials.

Dedication

To every dog professional out there, you are the reason behind this book. Your dedication, passion and unwavering commitment to improving the lives of dogs and their owners inspire us every single day. We hope you find within these pages the knowledge that acts as a key if you're feeling stuck and inspires you to keep moving forward.

Acknowledgements

We want to express our deepest gratitude to those who have supported us throughout this journey. Jo would like to thank her husband Darren and her boys Clay and Hudson. Your patience, support, belief and love have meant everything during the long hours we've spent away, focusing on the business and this book. Vicky extends her heartfelt thanks to Gareth, her husband and her guiding light. The rollercoaster of emotions experienced during this writing process has only made her stronger with his support. Both families' encouragement and belief in us have kept us going.

We also want to extend our sincere thanks to our mentors and everyone who has contributed to bringing this book to life. Your guidance, wisdom and support have been invaluable. To our readers, we hope the content within these pages reaches you and has the same profound effect on your lives as it has had on ours. Thank you for being a part of our journey.

Foreword

I recall vividly the day I told my mum I was going to be a dog trainer. She was furious. Those little lines above her twitching mouth furrowed and made her look old. She told me I had wasted years at university and begged me to at least explore the option of a vet nurse. Embarrassed that the neighbors might hear of this travesty through the walls, she whispered, "Come on Jo, you'll be poor forever. Me and your dad can't keep bailing you out of parking fines."

Mum, as it goes, was generally one of those people who was right about everything. She was right that form follows function, and so when you are creating something you should focus on what works; she was right that the mess in your home represents the mess in your head and that usually created a reflection of that mess in your heart; she was right that making lists meant things got done; and she was, of course, completely right that honey makes anything taste nice.

She was *not* right about my career choice.

I have been a dog trainer for nearly 20 years now: four prime time TV shows, countless appearances on things like *BBC News at Ten*, three published books and a three-time speaker in The Houses of Parliament. I've hosted hundreds of events worldwide, from New Zealand to across Europe and America, and hopefully this year, in Costa Rica. She wasn't right (sorry mum), but she nearly was.

When I first started, I was incredibly lucky. I found a job at a large animal charity, with well-managed infrastructure and some amazing mentors. But five or six years later, after I had completed all the qualifications I felt were necessary to charge people for money out on my own, I went rogue. I read on the internet that you should always include your location on your business name, so I did that and built my own website. Of course, my own dogs would be the logo. I printed t-shirts to wear and dropped leaflets at the vets. Boom. Clients came in and business was a go-go. And then, like we all do, I proceeded to make every single business mistake in the book. All the ones in this book and a fair few more.

Now, I am a reader, a listener and a learner by nature. I would be considered a "go-getter" and, as a result of my business knowledge shortcomings, I spent hours and hours (and hours and hours) reading business books, listening to podcast after podcast, downloading apps, listening to audiobooks, attending business seminars and learning with business coaches and life coaches. Now, I don't for a second regret that time, but damn! I wish this book had been available to buy then.

Jo and Vicky masterfully weave their own honest stories of mistakes and near-misses to create a book that isn't just full of "hahaha, I did that too!" moments. This book is also chock-full of "ah-ha!" moments. They have distilled hundreds of golden nuggets of advice I've received over the last 20 years into beautiful light bulb moments, all wrapped up in one dog business blueprint of a book. Not only that, but they have peppered it with tasks that make you want to grab your bookmark and start your business again from scratch. In fact, in the chapter about messaging, I called my website manager and told her to prepare herself for an entirely new copy for the website. This book shares a heartfelt story of two businesses that inspire you to improve your own offering and then lays out the steps and skills you need to make those changes.

Let's Talk Dog Business Strategy is a must-read for dog trainers. It describes a journey that most of us have taken, and in a way that fast-tracks the trainers of tomorrow while helping them miss the potholes that gave us all punctures and slowed us down. It is the first real book of its kind and one that I will be recommending to all of my dog trainer students. Jo and Vicky have managed to write a book that is funny, interesting and incredibly insightful, but not just that; it is a book that will make you want to get up off your bum and actually *do* the practical things that will improve your business, down to its very core foundations. Grab a cup of tea, a slice of cake, and a pen and pad, and enjoy.

Jo-Rosie Haffenden
World-renowned dog trainer, three-time published author and international speaker.

Contents

Introduction	1
Chapter 1 - Building Your Business	9
Chapter 2 - Mindset	29
Chapter 3 - Starting With Why	47
Chapter 4 - Core Business Principles	63
Chapter 5 - The Story of You	83
Chapter 6 - Your Niche, Your Genius	95
Chapter 7 - Nailing Your Offer	109
Chapter 8 - Messaging	121
Chapter 9 - Lead Generation	139
Chapter 10 - Sales	157
Conclusion	171
References	174
Testimonial	176

Introduction

You might be reading this book because you've just started a business or have owned one for quite some time. Either way, you're no doubt super keen and excited to implement core strategies aimed at propelling you to the next level and have your business operating in a way that is exciting and well thought-out. Deep down, you know that you and your business are destined for greatness; you just need to find out how to get past this feeling of being stuck. Have you got that fire in your belly burning so fiercely that you want to put your everything into making this work? We're with you. This is the fun bit! This is the bit where you get to see how your superpower of working with dogs can impact the world and your life. An even better bit? We know you're going to make it, it's going to work and it's going to give you the life you likely haven't even thought possible yet.

You might also be reading this book because you're a great dog trainer, but the business side of things is getting you down.

Perhaps you're overwhelmed with how much there is to do and feeling that there is never enough time to do it. Your expertise is dog training, not running a business!

You may be feeling close to burning out. Or are you perhaps earning far from a decent living? Working all of the hours available?

Is your home life being impacted from the pressures that come with running a business?

Or, maybe the passion and love that drove you to become a dog trainer in the first place is slowly dwindling and being replaced with resentment.

Are you feeling frustrated because deep down you know you've absolutely got this but are just feeling a bit stuck on which path to take at the moment?

Hi! We're Jo and Vicky, two dog trainers with a collective 27 years' experience running dog training and behaviour businesses. We came together to create Canine Business

Academy in 2023. We officially launched in January 2024, alongside our podcast *Let's Talk Dog Business,* where we delve into business strategies specifically for the dog industry. We are super passionate about bringing business expertise to the industry to improve the lives of people who work with dogs because we know how hard it can feel. We are so glad that you found us and we cannot wait to join you on this journey as you delve into the following pages.

By reading this book, you're going to learn everything you need to be able to implement the fundamental basics that are the foundational pillars of any successful business and design the dream life that works perfectly for you.

There are some caveats.

If you think the route to a healthy business strategy is a quick fix and all of your problems will disappear the instant you immerse yourself in the magic contained within these pages, then this book *isn't* for you.

If you pick and choose which pillars of the framework you work on and deviate from the order of implementation, then this book will *not* work for you.

If you don't spend time understanding the importance of each pillar fully, or you simply skim over them at surface level, then this book will *not* work for you.

This industry is amazing at providing a fantastic array of dog knowledge courses and mentorships to bump up our Continued Professional Development (CPD). Pretty much every specialism you can think of can be fully immersed in, thus allowing you to learn more, create a new type of service and pass it on to the most dedicated dog owners. We want to help educate and facilitate learnings that foster a strong desire to absolutely love what you do and feel confident in running a business, daunting as it may be.

For clarity, this book is not just about how to get more client enquiries and therefore more sales, although we don't deny this is absolutely essential and does play an integral part in the wider plan. We do cover that as well, don't worry. What this book is about, at its core, is teaching you the foundational building blocks, the nitty gritty of strategy that the rest of your business is built on.

When we set up our individual dog-training businesses many years ago, we mostly winged it and hoped for the best. No long-term plan was ever considered apart from creating a website, telling a few friends and family, waiting for the enquiries to come flooding in and sitting back to enjoy an idyllic dream life of working with dogs. Ha! If only! This is what anybody who *doesn't* work with dogs thinks, right? You are probably nodding along if one of the categories at the top of this introduction resonated with you.

A chance meeting led us to start conversations about the state of the industry and we quickly realised we shared identical views on the changes we felt needed to be made. Included in our list of changes are, for example, revolutionising archaic processes; expanding beliefs and mindsets within large and influential industry organisations (some of them accrediting); striving for better emotional support for trainers; reducing the feeling of fear of judgement from others; and equipping this profession with the best business knowledge available in order to positively impact the industry in a massive way.

Banded around a lot is that the industry has to be regulated to become the catalyst for any real improvement. While this is vital, we're not convinced this is the only way. We believe change, real change, needs to come from within. From you. From the ones who are living, breathing and working their damn hardest every single day for dogs and their owners.

Canine Business Academy (affectionately known as CBA) was formed with three beliefs at its core:

1. Dog trainers need to be valued more; firstly by themselves and then by the public.
2. Clients should be at the heart and soul of everything your business does.
3. Dogs deserve a better deal.

The order here is important. If dogs come first but you have low self-esteem and aren't viewed as professional, dogs ultimately lose out. If clients are put first but you aren't considering your needs and professionalism, you may run out of steam and again, the dogs lose out. As unnatural as it might seem to prioritise yourself and your own self-care, it could actually help towards serving and supporting your clients even better if your energy and vibrations are high.

Our passion for collaboration and connection is essential to create a true paradigm shift. We need one another as it's an impossible task for one person (or two in our case) to do it alone.

Our CBA clients have experienced and continue to experience life-changing results from working on themselves. Some have been inspired to ditch their paid employment jobs, some have hit financial goals within two months of working alongside us, some have gained more freedom and some have begun rebuilding strained relationships at home which were suffering as a result of business pressure.

This book will take you through the tried-and-tested pillars of our business basics framework. If applied properly, this framework will take you from where you currently are to where you'd like to be in your dog-training business.

We know more than most that implementing the work within this book can be a really bloody scary thing. Being pushed outside of your comfort zone and doing things you're not used to feels unnatural and vulnerable. Your body does a great job of trying to protect you and keep you safe, which is what may be stopping you from breaking the mould. Dog trainers generally mirror what others around them offer and charge, which is another reason for becoming stuck into feeling there is only one way of doing things.

Come with us on this journey of growth as you uncover the path less trodden and discover a place where there are no limits to your dog business. This is a journey where you can absolutely create whatever it is you want to do, however you want to do it and in your *own damn way*. This is your passion, your life and we're going to help you achieve your dream.

> *"If you change nothing, nothing changes."*
> – Joyce Brothers

Chapter 1
Building Your Business

An unshakable foundation will be the one thing that sets your business apart from others and it will help you weather any situation. Before we get into all the juicy bits that we strongly believe create these unshakable foundations, we want to set the scene and introduce you to how strategy and tactics are going to be a big part of how you now move forward.

Some of you reading this book may be thinking it will play out like a how-to guide with step-by-step actions that, when implemented, will make the big difference you're looking for. Whilst this is partly true, we want to iterate the importance of knowing what your overall strategy is before you implement any tactical elements. In these initial stages, it may feel like you're not doing anything worthwhile as there will be no immediate outcome.

Be patient. We're all about the results side of things as well, but trust us, this early work will be the most important thing you do for your business.

We're going to make a massive assumption and say that strategy isn't something a lot of us have in our businesses. We have had mixed experiences when it comes to strategizing. We both knew it was important. Jo probably had more of an insight with her background in marketing for big companies where strategy was always a strong focus. We think it's fair to say that for the majority of dog trainers and professionals out there, it's not something you would know how to do unless you've been shown how and even then it feels like a lot to wrap your head around.

It's easy to feel overwhelmed when thinking about a strategy for your own business. There are people out there shouting about all the tactical things you "should" be doing, such as Facebook Ads, Google Ads and how you need to be more present on social media. There's funnel marketing and how it's important to have lead magnets that drive people to your funnels. There's business coaching from various different aspects, additional lead generation tactics, sales skills (although oddly we haven't seen much of this for the dog industry).

Build a community, don't build a community, build an email list, build a phone list, create a passive income revenue stream (that's a biggie in 2024). There's even AI technology aimed at dog businesses now. Wherever you turn, there is something to remind you about all the things you "should" be doing for your business, yet it's unclear where to start. Don't worry, we've totally got you covered. If that feeling of being overwhelmed creeps back in, just pop it back down for a moment; all will become clear.

This is possibly in part due to you thinking all the above "things" are the "how" you implement your plan and are all therefore necessary, rather than first working on and knowing your overarching plan. This leads to feeling like there's just too much to do and you become paralysed by the inability to make decisions or you go and spend time, energy and money to do all of the "things" mentioned, ultimately achieving nothing. You must first decide on a strategy, then lay down tactics or ways to achieve it.

Truth is, you may have yet to lay down the fundamental foundational work that this book will cover, which is where the feeling of being stuck is coming from. Winging it is 100% something we've been brilliant at in the past. Heck, we even wore it as a badge of honour that we were able to make profit and deliver client sessions with little to no planning, usually at the expense of our sanity and with a whole lot of anxiety. This is not the best foundation for any business in the long-term and certainly something we've had to work hard on to change!

When you're looking at all the advertisements and listening to all the people talk about the millions of ways you could conduct your business, it seems logical and sensible enough. You could definitely do all that, you might have told yourself, yet when it comes down to it, our brains switch off and everything goes out the window. Standing in front of all those choices and all those possibilities, you realise that you are now responsible for everything. Every success and every mess starts and ends with you. In some ways, you think this could work for you. You're the only one who's going to know what's really going on and you could take the easy route and just wing it. And this might just work. You could dabble in it all and see what sticks by taking each day as it comes and just seeing what happens. There's no denying it worked for us for several years! The best reinforcement there is going! No plan, yet somehow we made money! Easy. And so the cycle repeats.

Let us break down strategy and tactics in a way that allowed us to work smarter, not harder and enabled us to have the thriving businesses we have today.

What Is a Business Strategy?

Simply put, a strategy is a road map towards reaching your goals. Imagine putting an end destination into a sat nav and it comes up with a big question mark on how to get there. That's you with your goals but without a strategy. Or let's say you decide to go on holiday to America. Amazing! You know where you're going, just not how to get there. You see, you can't just buy a plane ticket to America. You have to pick a certain part you want to visit, choose how long you're staying and what best to do while you're there, all according to the budget you set. Those are the big things. Then there are the little details and questions to ask. Are the passports in date? Do the dogs need boarding whilst you're away? Which boarding establishment will you use? How are you going to get to the airport?

We acknowledge this example might seem far-fetched, however, it's a point we want to illustrate because there's a good majority of us that do not have this awareness in our business. And it's the business that is going to ensure whether you can continue doing what you love and bring the money in to pay for bills, food and all the things you want in life.

Every day you might be feeling like you're winging it and hoping for the best. We are on a schedule of random reinforcement which keeps us addicted to this way of working. We surround ourselves with other people who confirm our inner thoughts – whether good or bad – and we'll seek the affirmations we're looking for and absolutely find them.

This needs to change.

We need to design and create the route to get to the end destination.

Strategy is the plan that combines all of the potential routes and actions you could take for the business to achieve its purpose and puts them together in an easy-to-follow roadmap. It looks at the inside and outside of your business, such as perspectives from others, and the strengths and weaknesses of the business in comparison to the market as a whole. This allows you to really get under the hood of your business to truly understand it and how this is all going to work. Strategy allows you to look at the best routes possible, giving you different alternatives based on cost, speed and effectiveness. It allows you to stand strong when external forces come along and shake something up. It's really not too dissimilar to the sat nav example when you think about it.

Where Do Tactics Come in?

Tactics are the actionable steps to help you achieve your strategy, providing details on how you're going to get there. They could also be referred to as your micro strategies because each part of your bigger picture goal is broken down into smaller projects to help see you get there. Remember, these are the things that you do to support the overall strategy. So, if you are wanting to be known as the go-to person in your local area yet you start working on an online programme for passive income, these two things do not align and will not work in synergy. An online programme may get you passive income from a wider reach of audience, yes, but it will take you away from your bigger goal of becoming known in your own area first.

Some examples of how strategy and tactics blend together:

- **Example 1**

  Strategy Goal (What): Gain 100 new clients in a 12-month period

  Tactics (How):

  - Build an email list.
  - Make press appearances.
  - Focus on the social media platform that has the highest amount of engagement.
  - Collaborate with other businesses to target their audience also.
  - Put on an event or workshop to gain followers.
  - Send emails to target customers.

- **Example 2**

  Strategy Goal (What): Increase followers on Instagram platform by 30% in a 12-month period

  Tactics (How):

  - Create a social media campaign that will attract attention and engagement.
  - Run social media ads for awareness.

- Connect with others that have a large audience and find a way to do a combined live or posts where each of you are being tagged.
- Increase the number of posts to 20 a week.
- Repurpose old content.

Applying the tactics to the strategy now makes it easier to execute. The best way to do this is by doing something fancy called reverse engineering, which essentially means that you pick your destination (the goal) and then write down all the ways you believe you could get there. Get creative and think outside the box. List down all the possibilities and then you'll see which ones feel right for the task. It doesn't have to be perfect, but it's a start.

Once you have these, the next step is to map out exactly what the step details. For example, where it states build an email list, let's get clearer. We need to consider:

- How many emails are we aiming for?
- Where are we going to get them from?
- Do we need to create a lead magnet?
- What needs to be on that lead magnet?
- Who are we targeting?
- Where are we going to store the email addresses?

Strategy and tactics must work hand-in-hand to ensure everything aligns and to avoid you going off on a tangent.

You can't operate a successful business without knowing your strategy. It's the fuel of the business. You could wing it, as other businesses have, but this won't work if you want yours to last. Inevitably, you'll reach a point of burnout which we know is so common in this industry. It's not sustainable to keep doing all the stuff, working all the hours and living month-to-month not knowing if you're going to be able to afford the bills.

This industry has lost some amazing people over the last couple of years due to frustration, burnout and a sense of disheartenment working with clients. The amount of threads posted all over social media are really saddening to see when the passion, desire and love for dogs is so high and yet people cannot make this profession work well for them.

This is why a change in direction is needed now. Creating a strategy to sustain your business will give the stability that you crave. We're all dog folk; we all know about the lizard part of the brain that just wants to feel safe. Let's feed that bit so that the creative part can go in full flow and deliver awesome services to the dogs.

We've both hit points in our career where we have felt completely defeated by everything. The following are just some examples:

- Not getting enough enquiries.
- Not attracting the right clients.
- Not having enough time to do all the stuff because we're too busy with the delivery.
- Not having a core product and therefore having loads of different services.
- Fear of not getting any business so created something for everyone.
- No goals.
- Not knowing what we were working towards.
- No idea where the next bit of money was coming from.
- Not making a living wage.
- Cash flow in the business was rubbish.

In order to avoid these breakdowns on your journey to the end destination – sticking with the example of the sat nav – we need to figure out the best route to help us achieve the goal. Everything a business does should answer or heed to the reason it exists in the first place.

Let's look at an example of what we have both offered over the years, which is also the typical offerings of your usual dog business nowadays. We both spent the first stages of our business poring over the name and logo, spending more time than necessary on them. And when it came to thinking about what our business would actually offer, well it pretty much became all of it at once:

- Puppy classes
- Adolescent classes
- Scent classes
- Agility classes
- Hoopers classes
- Obedience classes
- 1:1s
- Behavioural consults
- Reactivity 1:1s
- Reactivity classes
- Social walks
- Training walks
- Trained for you
- Board and train
- Loose lead workshop
- Recall workshop
- Dog first-aid days

After deciding we could totally do all that, we went on to tell everyone we knew about our businesses, publishing social media posts about us being dog trainers and generally just trying to drum up clients in haphazard ways. We created social media business accounts on several platforms and started posting the odd video or picture and shared some information about dogs. We spent time in local area Facebook groups waiting to jump on a post to recommend ourselves when someone asked, "Does anyone offer dog training or puppy classes?" Then hey-ho we landed our first enquiry.

Emails were sent back stating all the reasons why they should pick us and only then did we realise we needed to price ourselves. We didn't want to seem too expensive so we had a quick look at some other trainers in the area and got stuck with thoughts of going in the middle or lower to appear more appealing. We also didn't want to come across as salesy so we stressed that they had the choice on how many sessions they wanted to go ahead with.

Huzzah! Someone said yes! And the cycle repeated.

Whilst in those early days we were running separate businesses to each other, the story was pretty much the same. Once those first enquires came in, we were making it up as we went along. We hadn't thought about processes for taking payment and even the thought of asking for money filled us with dread. However, we each stumbled through those first few bookings and got trapped in the cycle while the businesses (we use this term lightly) ended up growing and sustaining us for a while.

There are some fond memories when we look back at those days. Without a strategy, those first few years were way harder than they had to be, but at the very least we're thankful because it taught us exactly what not to do. Many sleepless nights and anxiety-filled days stemmed from the fact that winging it was the only way we knew how to do our businesses.

Jo recalls several times that certain clients would say they'd pay cash at the session, only for them to come up with excuses for not paying after the service had been carried out. Needless to say, it did absolutely nothing for her self-esteem and the shame of going home to explain she'd done a day's work for literally nothing was soul-destroying. Not knowing exactly what we were doing and muddling along figuring everything out as we went definitely took its toll on home life for both of us.

Comments such as, "Why don't you just go and get a proper job and put all this behind you" and "Is it really worth it?" echoed loudly most weeks. A lack of strategy does absolutely nothing for your self-esteem.

The lack of strategy and getting the business fundamentals right makes your entire business a haphazard one. It is our belief that there are many trainers out there, you may even feel like this is you, that started their business in a similar way and so we feel it our duty to let you know it doesn't have to be like that. Avoid all the pitfalls we made. Creating a roadmap to plan out the exact route to how you're going to achieve your goals is crucial. There is not a successful business out there that does not have a strategy in place. Your strategy may not be perfect and we're all only human and can only take on so much, but there *has* to be a strategy.

When we both took action and decided to run our businesses like a business, we sat down and created a strategy using the steps in this book to help us get there. Within the first 12 months of doing this work, our businesses soared. We were spending more time at home, having better quality relationships with clients, seeing better results and our income increased to levels we never dreamed possible. We both take messy, imperfect actions to get us one step closer to being better at how we apply these techniques. Without taking action and using the information in this book, Canine Business Academy would never have come to fruition. It would have never soared to global-business status within the first 14 weeks of its existence, accompanied by a top-ranked podcast to boot.

Hopefully by now you're starting to realise a few things. First, we're a bit passionate about this stuff! And second, you need to start thinking differently about your business. So let's get stuck in and get going on creating a strategy that works for you.

Get Your SWOT on

To begin creating a strategy for your business, we recommend starting by conducting a SWOT analysis which stands for Strengths, Weaknesses, Opportunities and Threats. This exercise can be carried out whichever stage of business you're at. A SWOT analysis means looking at your business' strengths, weaknesses, opportunities and threats. This is a powerful framework to take the greatest possible advantage of all opportunities out there and is something that top performing companies will complete on a regular basis.

The two main reasons you would use this framework is to look at the services you offer, as well as to understand the marketplace. If you've never done this before, start with a broader look at your business and how it's positioned in your marketplace. Your marketplace could be your local area, or if you're looking to enter the online space, then it's looking much further afield about what is already out there.

The following grid gives you an idea of what questions to ask and answer in each section when looking at this from a prospective customer view:

Strengths	**Weaknesses**
Identify the advantages that you have. What do you do better than your rivals? What perception does a client or competitor assume about your business?	What do your competitors do better than you? What do you do poorly? What processes can you improve?

Opportunities	**Threats**
Where can you apply your strengths? How are your clients' needs changing? How do you incorporate current trends and technology?	Are customers able to get the same as what you offer elsewhere? Is the perception to your customers that they'll get better service elsewhere? Are your customers' needs changing? Is your competition faster at adapting than you? Think of threats that are coming. For example, when the bully breed ban came in, how would this impact your business and what needs to happen? Industry regulations. How much of a threat is this? Is there a timeline? What do you need to work towards?

A strength we had with our dog-training businesses is that we had each been established long enough that our neighbourhoods had positive opinions of our services.

Some weaknesses included a period of time when we reached capacity really quickly as it was only us handling our businesses.

When looking at opportunities and threats, think about collaborations you could explore with others in your area that could then be turned into an opportunity. Just be mindful of anything that could cause harm to your business. A big threat that took everybody by surprise was the global pandemic. We can now add this into our threats box because we know it's happened before and could happen again. It was a really good example because most industries all reacted spontaneously as there was little planning for an event like that.

By starting to look at the bigger picture and having more awareness about your business, you are on the start of your journey to making amazing things happen. Start with this exercise and then think about your end goal for the next 12 months and what you would like to achieve in this time. It could be things like gaining 100 new clients, increasing your annual revenue to a specific target amount or even giving yourself your time back to spend with family. Think about what you're going to need to do to reach these goals and have fun popping all ideas down on a piece of paper or on a device. Then run those ideas through your SWOT analysis to see how they could play out. It could be that you decide to stop offering adolescent classes, how does that impact the business? A threat could be it reduces income, a strength could be it gives you more time back to dedicate to something else that is more in line with where you want the business to be going. Once you've done this exercise do not pop it away, keep it out because you're going to want to refer back to it as you layer in the coming chapters.

Let's take some messy, imperfect action together now and go all in on creating a thriving business you are proud of and love!

Chapter 2
Mindset

It might seem strange having a section called mindset in a book about how to grow, scale and fall in love with your dog business. But we promise you, having the wrong mindset is just as much of a pitfall as lacking a strategy. It is the reason why, after investing in all the courses, including our CPD, that we still feel like imposters and don the imposter syndrome badge and live and breathe this view of ourselves. It is the reason why, when a new trainer pops up in your local area, you feel instantly like you're resource-guarding your business. It is the reason why you feel frustrated with your clients and are able to rant about how non-compliant they are. It is the one skill in life you actually have control of, but that you may not have mastered yet. No matter what business strategies you implement, it's bound to fail if you haven't got the right mindset.

Mindset is one of those words that get banded around a lot. However, no one really teaches you how your mindset can have both a positive and negative impact on running your dog business. We all focus more of our time and energy on learning about dogs and therein lies the problem. You love dogs and you love geeking out on new courses; it lights you up and releases that hit of dopamine that studying business and forming a mindset maybe doesn't. As human beings, we generally actively avoid anything that we feel is too difficult or anything we've proclaimed as not being for us.

Unfortunately, this is why the dog industry is now thought of as being in shambles in certain circles. And it isn't just us professionals who suffer because of this opinion; it is impacting the industry we love as a whole because the public no longer views us as a professional industry to begin with. If it continues on this trajectory, then you may not get to work with dogs anymore. A big corporate company could easily come in and take over, resulting in no more need for solo dog trainers. A bit extreme perhaps, but also possibly not far from the truth.

We want you to really lean in on this chapter because this lays the foundations for the rest of the book. We want you to be open minded and look at this chapter as a means of introducing some new ideas to you or, indeed, reiterating ideas you may have heard previously. By studying this chapter fully, you will start to change some of those pathways in your brain and realise some deep profound shit about yourself. It won't be easy and it may not always be fun. But come the other side, we promise you it will allow you to start the business journey you're looking for. This is where it gets exciting.

What Is Mindset?

The English Oxford dictionary definition of mindset states "the established set of attitudes held by someone."

Your mindset is made up of a collection of beliefs that are formed primarily by your childhood experiences and upbringing. It affects how you navigate and experience the world, as well as the way you respond to each and every situation encountered. Your thoughts, your feelings and your behaviour are all influenced by mindset and the cool part is, you can totally change how you think, feel and act on something. The main question is, are you willing to change it so that you can open up possibilities in your life that you never thought were achievable?

A quick search on Google or social media will quickly return results from several mindset coaches that claim to embrace a more purposeful, passion-filled and empowered existence (that's a whole lot of P's!) and similar, but is it really necessary to invest in a mindset coach or invest your time into learning this craft? Let's deep dive for a moment...

One way to view mindset is on the surface level where there are two main types, commonly labelled as a fixed mindset or a growth mindset. According to Stanford Psychologist Carol Dweck,[1] a fixed mindset may limit success due to the inability to change outlooks or attitudes to situations presented. A lack of effort may also be evident if a person perceives their talent and intelligence as valuable enough to achieve greatness. Somebody with a growth mindset however, is always open to learning new ways of doing things to help them develop and evolve. A persistent amount of effort is also usually evident in this type of person as they work hard to achieve their goals by adapting.

Essentially, if you feel you're the type of person who will always find excuses to not do something, or has very strong opinions on something and are not always willing to be open to conversations as you're always right, you're living in a fixed mindset. If, on the other hand, you find yourself keen to learn more and often step out of your comfort zone a lot, then you likely have a growth mindset.

Great! But how on earth does this impact your business? Look at the following table, which lists some thoughts or phrases you might be hearing yourself say as a dog trainer on a regular basis:

Fixed Mindset	**Growth Mindset**
"I've always trained dogs this way, and I'm not changing now."	"I'm open to learning new skills to improve my training skills."
"I'm not good at marketing; I'll never get more clients."	"Marketing is a skill I can learn and improve to attract more clients."
"I don't have enough time to run my business and train dogs."	"I can find ways to manage my time better and do both tasks."
"I'm afraid to raise my prices; clients will leave and no one wants to pay them."	"Raising my prices can reflect the value I provide, and I can attract clients who appreciate that."

"If the dog doesn't respond right away, it means I'm not good at this."	"If the dog doesn't respond right away, it's an opportunity to try a different approach."
"I can't compete with established trainers in my area."	"I can offer unique services and build my reputation to stand out in my area."
"If I fail at a business venture, it means I'm not cut out for this."	"Every failure is a learning experience that can help me improve my business."
"I've reached my limit in what I can achieve with my business."	"There's always room for growth. I can find new opportunities to expand my business."
"It's the client's fault if the dog doesn't improve because they don't listen."	"I can communicate more effectively and find strategies to motivate clients to follow through."
"If clients don't follow the plan, there's no point in trying."	"I can adjust the plan to make it more manageable and achievable for clients."

If whilst reading the fixed mindset column you were thinking, "Yup, that's me! But it's true!" then firstly, see how that in itself is fixed? And secondly, don't worry at all. You're absolutely not a lost cause.

Vicky struggled hugely with her mindset while developing her business over the years. At the time, she wasn't even aware of just how much her mindset was impacting her choices and outcomes. Vicky has a mix of fixed and growth mindsets in some respects, as we all do. She always had a fiercely passionate drive to do the best in business right from the beginning, stemming from her clear purpose. However, alongside this, she also had a set of principles instilled in her from a young age: a solid work ethic that meant she excelled and thrived well in a team, a fierce loyalty and a determination to never let colleagues or friends down. Whilst all of this might sound awesome, the reality was her mindset was so fixed that she couldn't sway from these principles, and it caused problems further down the line.

Going back a bit, at the age of 15 earning £2.80 every hour (yes, we are that old!) in an after-school waitressing job, Vicky was single handedly responsible for feeding and clearing up an average of 50 tables, as well as making salad garnish starters, keeping the bread and butter table topped up and preparing the desserts. Generous tips from the regulars were a partial driver in wanting to provide an awesome service – we are talking 1996, so generous was actually £1 here and there! Though she was not yet even aware of this mindset malarkey at the time, Vicky already had elements of a growth mindset appearing with the belief that customers come first. Anything that could be done to improve their day were actions to be taken. Contending with this was a fixed mindset element: a belief that she could only move within the parameters she had been given. This was the role and she had to play it out the exact way the boss had prescribed.

Fast forward 12 years to 2008, Vicky had been running her own fledgling dog-training business for a full year. This was a pivotal point where she began adding countless additional services to "complement" her core puppy class offering. The reason all these services had been added was due to a fixed mindset. If you look back over the examples previously given you can see this playing out here. There was a belief somewhere that offering puppy classes was not enough; it wasn't what people wanted and these people wanted more. There was a belief about income not being enough, therefore the need to create more opportunities to create more income and attract more clients was prevalent.

The decision to add more was not from a place of growth, but a place of fear. No matter what you tell yourself about the decision to add in services or how you feel about a given situation, 99% will always come from a place of uncertainty and fear when you operate in a fixed mindset.

Another way to look at fixed mindsets is that they are the beliefs you have that do not serve you. In other words, you can convince yourself not to go ahead with something because of a belief or a story you feel is true, whether or not you've got evidence for it. We refer to these thoughts as limiting beliefs.

Examples include:

- "People won't buy from me if I'm more expensive than other trainers in the area." This is a limiting money mindset belief.
- "A new trainer that has popped up in my area has more dog knowledge and skills than me." Good old imposter syndrome acting up.
- "A new trainer in your area doesn't have enough knowledge or qualifications, or doesn't have genuine intentions." This is a fixed mindset.
- "Why would people buy from me over X who offers X?" Imposter syndrome again.

- "I should avoid investing in my business during uncertain times." This limits growth.
- "People want everything for free." This is a limiting belief.

These beliefs are so damn common in dog trainers! You only have to look at dog-trainer-specific social media groups to see the overarching theme of negativity. Thread after thread of client bashing, jealousy, suspicion, cynicism; you name it, it's there. No wonder trainers are scared to ask for help, or post anything that could possibly be misunderstood or taken out of context. God help the backlash! These groups are full of tonnes and tonnes of fixed mindsets all stemming from fear.

Every conversation with the amazing industry professionals we've had the pleasure to collaborate with have all landed on a common theme. The industry is letting its people down with a complete and utter lack of support. We have heard it described as a shambles, a failure and a crisis to name but a few. How bloody bleak. The worst part about all of this? Those you surround yourself with are likely impacting your fixed mindset and limiting beliefs. It's likely that any time you try to step out of the "norm" or try to grow yourselves and your business, there is always someone who loves you in your life that will express their concern for you. Or if it isn't someone in your circle, it's you feeding your limiting beliefs by spending time in social media groups that pin it all on the clients or the like. If others are experiencing this, and feel the same blameless way, then of course it must be true.

This will never help you grow.

This is something we are big, in fact, HUGE on. You are the average of the five people you spend the most time with. If those five people happen to have a fixed mindset, guess what, this will start affecting your beliefs and you are likely to act and think like them. There is even evidence to suggest that you will have an average of each other's salaries. Makes sense when you really think about it. You don't typically see millionaires spending all their time and energy on people who are striving for £18,000 each year. So imagine what spending more time with people who really want to make a change and do amazing things with their life and business could do for you.

The thing here is to be mindful of who gets your time and energy, of others' fixed and growth mindsets and how that impacts you directly. Both of us have strong personality types in our lives in the form of friends and family, so when it comes to fixed mindsets, we are aware of the drain on our energy and motivation when we are around these people. It's not a case of suddenly cutting them from your life because, let's face it, some of those people are likely to be your family. It's about being aware and introducing ways to combat it.

Some things that work really well for us include stating positive outcomes of the day just passed and doing this daily for a few weeks. It could be doing some physical exercise before you see the person you know has a miserable attitude and is always negative. Steer clear of certain social media groups if you find yourself reaching for the keyboard to write negatively about an experience. We talk a lot with each other about our thoughts and feelings on things and challenge one another a lot to identify where that thought has come from, i.e. decide whether it is fact or something we've told ourselves to be true. We invest heavily in surrounding ourselves with people we strive to be and commonly joke that some of our best friends now are the ones we have paid for. The more you can control your awareness of what is feeding your mindset, the better chance you have of using it as a superpower. Try answering this: How do you look at growth when confronted with it? Do you get excited, or are you shit scared?

Austrian neurologist, psychologist, philosopher and Holocaust survivor Vicktor Frankl is famously quoted for saying, "Between stimulus and response there is a space. In that space is our power to choose the response. In our response lies our growth and our freedom."

This is a powerful statement because it suggests that when you start to do some work on your triggers and autopilots, you can start to find better solutions to the problems you and your business face. Working from the inside out to make these changes may seem illogical in the first instance, but think of it like building a house on dodgy foundations. It will stay up for a little while for sure, but without the correct structure cementing the building blocks in, the walls will gradually give way to a crumbled mess.

Laying strong foundations within yourself is equally as important as laying the foundations for the business. We just don't think it is possible to do one without the other. If Canine Business Academy had formed whilst our individual journeys of personal growth were still in early stages of progress, we can categorically guarantee the following: We wouldn't have a Number 1 podcast. We wouldn't have written this book. We wouldn't have created our results-driven courses and programmes. We wouldn't have formed the most amazing collaborative partnerships we have done so far. All that is because we concentrated on creating rock solid footings. The tools to craft them have been passed on to us like a baton in a relay race by our own mentors, and we now want to pass these on to you.

Mindset is a gradual journey and not one that can be implemented in a quick minute. The ability to not only bounce back when things get tough, but to have more clarity on your business and even more confidence and belief in yourself, is invaluable.

Instead of viewing what you deem failures as a weakness, flipping them into opportunities to learn and grow will foster a growth mindset to catapult your hunger and vision for making a positive impact. Think of resilience as a muscle that needs flexing. The downs of life and business, although at the time can absolutely seem like the world is against you, is in fact allowing you a chance to exercise the strength and determination required to succeed and overcome adversity a little easier next time.

Resilience is a skill, a mindset, a lifestyle, much like joining a gym and sticking to the new habit of commitment it asks of us. Although Vicky had earlier learnt some really useful foundational skills from her roles in the hospitality industry, she did struggle to transfer all of the elements into running her own business and, of course, all of the stress and uncertainty that comes with it. Let's use the analogy of a dog's inability to generalise training to every environment and scenario initially. It takes dedicated reps and consistency to achieve success to get there.

You could start working on changing your mindset by spending time with yourself and asking these questions:

- What do I think is currently holding me back in my business?
- If there was no fear or judgement, what would I be doing with my life and business?
- What thoughts and phrases do I find myself thinking and saying on a regular basis?
- Are these even my thoughts?
- Where could they have come from?
- What evidence supports these thoughts?

For example, if you believe you have imposter syndrome and find yourself leaning in on this thought, then write down some facts. If you believe you have imposter syndrome on your dog-training ability look to your current clients and dogs, are they achieving results? Are you getting good reviews? Do people refer and recommend you? Have you got evidence of achieving knowledge? The idea here is that the more you can talk with your brain to tell itself that there is evidence supporting the opposite of your limiting belief, it will gradually start to go away. The more you tell your brain that there is evidence against a limiting belief, the less you'll believe it.

We've previously mentioned about who you spend your time around. This is an incredibly tricky one and one that is an ongoing journey because of its growth. Start small and spend some time in a different social media group perhaps, or switch off channels that feed the negativity. Hide certain people on social media so that it's not an instant "unfriending" action, just a nice little hide-away so you can focus on you. You could even try reading some books on something completely different and learning about something new.

We took this to a whole new level and immersed ourselves in law of attraction and manifesting books because of the positive thought processes that go along with it.

The key to mindset is that it's not a case of "do this and this will happen." It is a continuous journey. Finding something you can do daily will really help. Another thing you could do is write down all the things that went really well that day before you go to sleep. This shouldn't just be work specific, but everything about that day.

You could include things like, the sun shone, you had fuel in your car to get you about, you had food in the fridge, a significant other gave you a hug, a dog you were working with did something incredible today and recalled from a situation you'd been working towards. Doing this work really helps retrain your brain to become more growth oriented.

This may feel a bit weird in the first instance; we'd be lying if we said we didn't struggle with this when we first adopted this practice. However, it's now something we cannot go without doing.

Over these coming chapters, you will see whether you've got a fixed mindset or a growth one depending on how you respond to the suggestions.

Own your awareness and try to lean in on a bit of growth. Ultimately, this is exactly why you're here. You've got nothing to lose and so much to gain.

Chapter 3
Starting With Why

"Why?" Seems like a really bloody obvious question right? Why did you create your business? Perhaps it was because you love dogs? Seems fair. But what specifically made you think that loving dogs equalled a business? Or perhaps you didn't even necessarily think of starting a business and just thought working with dogs would be fun. Maybe you landed yourself a job in another dog-related role and thought you could do this, or maybe you had an experience with training and thought you could do better? Maybe it just totally lit a fire in your belly and made you want to do this. We hear you. You're not the only one in a position like this. In fact, collectively we both had similar experiences to those listed above in starting our journey into dog training, but ended up taking very different paths to where we are today.

So "Why?" may sound like a completely bonkers question to ask. You may be wondering what on earth this has to do with running a business that is successful, you are proud of and enjoy working on every single day. Answering the why really helps craft and create the foundations of what you do. It allows every single action you take to be aligned with what you are trying to achieve in your business. So many people in this industry will answer with "I do it because I love dogs." In fact, in a survey we ran in December 2023, 34% answered with you do what you do because you love dogs, followed by 20% of those people wanting to improve the lives of dogs and then joint third, each with 11%, was improving the lives of owners and thinking of preventative strategies for owners and problems for dogs.

Already you can start to see a pattern emerge, which may not come as much of a shock to you. You all love dogs! On our podcast, *Let's Talk Dog Business*, we interviewed Kelly Gorman-Dunbar, who suggested that people go into this industry for lucrative reasons, assuming they know how to run a business. Now of course there is context around this, and you'll have to go and check out the *Let's Talk Dog Business* podcast to find out more about that. It was an interesting point because where we are in the UK, it's certainly not the thought that many people entered into this industry for the money. If anything, there seems to be a common theme that it is impossible to make a living wage out of running a dog business unless you cram your diary with every single spare hour possible and offer a million services. There's even an idea of it being "dirty" for you to earn a decent living from doing dog training or anything to do with dogs. It is our strong belief that one of your whys should absolutely factor in making a decent earning from your business. You still have to pay your bills, do your CPD, feed your family and be the emotional support system for all the dog owners out there who require your services. It's a bloody challenging job. Without a why and without a living wage, it becomes very difficult to run your business effectively.

Answering "Why?" is a starting point you should all revisit, or even visit for the first time if you've never done this work before, to ensure you have a solid answer to that question. It's also important to note that it is absolutely okay and totally normal for your why to change as you continue to grow in your business. And in actual fact, it should change.

When Jo started in this industry in 2014, she wasn't even 100% sure what it was that made her go into it. She'd gotten her first ever dog in her adult years. She was that deprived child who grew up with no pets – apart from a guinea pig she managed to persuade her parents to let her get when she was 12 – so went all in and adopted a Siberian Husky. Her parents refused to speak to her for over two weeks even though she had her own house and the dog would be nowhere near them or their household things (extreme, right?). Jo was as stubborn as ever, knowing that she was going to make this work when everyone around her was telling her she was a fool for getting this breed of dog.

It makes us laugh now because, 10 years later, we can hear ourselves saying internally, "OMG. What on earth are you doing!" whenever someone rings saying they have a husky and it's their first dog. Oh, the irony. However, we're actually doing these clients a massive disservice with thoughts like this. Jo certainly pisses herself off whenever she thinks that on a reflex because it's actually not her thought, it's everybody else's that has become so deeply ingrained in our belief system that it's an automatic thought response. We annoy ourselves for having that thought because we were once like them with our own dogs and, as cliché as it sounds, we may not be here doing what we do now if we hadn't gotten our dogs. When we find ourselves thinking in stereotypes, we remind ourselves that we don't know enough about the person and their determination or desire for what's to follow on their dog-owning or training journey.

Cue Sunday morning Kennel Club obedience training classes on a cricket field with approximately four to five more classes taking place at the same time, all priced at £2 per session – crazy! The star of this show? Jo and her husky Laika. They attended for about six months to complete a six-week course that cost a total of £60, not counting some fees for separate sessions. Jo and Laika did pretty well, with Jo enjoying spending time with her first dog and getting to see what she could do – until frustration set in, as expected in any set up like this. Other people were getting ahead, others were trailing behind and with only one instructor for a class of 15, Jo found herself getting annoyed. First, it was the set-up that got her gears grinding, then she started getting frustrated at how Laika wasn't performing as well as Jo knew she could. So Jo's pure elation and pride at her first dog came mixed with moments of embarrassment, annoyance and feeling like a terrible trainer.

Frustrating as they were, these feelings absolutely fueled the fire to create the why for the business that would eventually follow.

When Jo looks back now she can definitely say she learnt a lot from that experience. Jo had gotten the training bug and wanted to continue as soon as humanly and physically possible (she's a bit impatient). So she invested in a private 1:1 trainer for 12-months for her and Laika, realising very quickly that this wasn't going to work for her and had essentially been a waste of money. All this was happening at a time when dog training on TV was quite big with what seemed to be extreme cases of dog behaviour being fixed in minutes by truly understanding what the dog was trying to tell you or how you as the human need to behave and act around a dog. Or so it was positioned. We shan't dwell on what all that was about, nonetheless it piqued Jo's interest into this fascinating world of dogs and there she began her journey. She cannot honestly say that she did it because she loved dogs in the generic sense, but she loved Laika and the bond they were creating. Add in the fact that she'd always been obsessed with psychology, so diving into animal psychology seemed right up her street.

Needless to say, the following year was dedicated to learning all she could about dogs alongside an incredibly hectic corporate job in the ad agency world (if you know, you know), and dabbling with seeing "clients" to help them on their way with their dog. In reality it was more like test-driving the skills she'd been learning from afar to see if they worked and if she was any good at helping others! It was a bit of a shit show really, but one we both now know to be how a good percentage of this industry started, or at least did back then. Whilst the knowledge element in industry has certainly improved now, the business side is still severely lacking and needs urgent attention.

Experian data collected in 2023 shows that 50% of new startup businesses fail within the first three years[2] and we strongly believe this is because business strategy is not being followed. There isn't a strong enough reason these businesses exist to base the strategy on.

The why that Jo's business was initially based on was curiosity and enjoyment of working with dogs and doing something new that didn't require the same brain cells she had been using for the past 13 years in the agency world. There was certainly not a clear strategic why and it showed.

She showed up in the only way she knew how: by promising to fix things she didn't know how to fix, thinking it would be great learning. Offering one-off sessions for £10, later increasing to £30 (this industry seems to love £30 sessions), hoping to drum up enough business to see if she could make it viable to leave her £60,000 salary job with a company car and the title of Account Director – something she had strived to achieve before turning 30. Sidenote: She managed this at 29 and was so bloody chuffed with herself! But hoping to make that salary was literally all she could do because she certainly had no plan on how she was going to achieve it. She just assumed that one day, if she kept plugging away, then it might, maybe, possibly happen. Why on earth did she want to do this dog-training business? She still had no answer and kept going.

Because she didn't know her why, which meant she didn't know the how and was only looking at it from a point of view of trying to match her salary, she stayed in that corporate job for longer than she initially wanted. When she looks back now, it's clear to her it was because she had no reason she was doing what she was doing and therefore had no real motivation to leave. The money was steady and it's what we're told and brought up to believe: Landing a good career is what life is supposed to be about. She had the fancy car, the aspirational senior position in a large company and the decent salary. She wonders if, subconsciously, she thought she would never be able to replace this income – certainly not with £30 sessions! The lack of a why meant she had no motivation to ramp things up. Not knowing why she truly wanted to pursue this dog-training journey meant she was going in blind and nothing flowed from it.

Now, it's not impossible to have some success running a business this way, because it certainly did the job for her in those early years. However, she 100% couldn't really call it a business because she wasn't running it like one; she was winging it! All of this hung on the fact that she didn't know why she was doing what she was doing.

"Why" is the reason you get up every morning and do what you do. Why is knowing that every decision you make in your business and for your clients and all the dogs you see is edging you one step closer every day to the reason you do what you do. Why is how you can measure some part of your own success story. The why is your story, and we can assure you, your story is one people want to hear.

It's worth noting again that your why may change from the original reason and that is 100% okay and normal. It is worth sitting down and thinking about why you originally got into this business even if it was a bit of a hobby and you just loved dogs. It will help you realise just how much you've grown already on your journey in being an entrepreneur.

Where do you even begin on trying to figure this out? Carve out some time to reflect on your time in business and have a look at the following questions and see what answers come up for you:

1. Identify your successes and failures. Are there any patterns?
2. What does the business care about the most?
3. What other businesses or people inspire you?
    a. Why is this?
    b. How do you see this emulating in your business?

4. Think about the impact you want to have by running your business. Try answering some of these questions:
   a. How do you want customers to feel when they work with you?
   b. What would you like people to be saying about you?
   c. What lights you up when you get to deliver it?
5. Imagine you closed the doors to the business now. What do you think people would remember you for? Would you be remembered? (Ouch, this one hits home!).
6. If you were to sell the business, what is someone buying that isn't the tangible things? They're buying the idea, remember.

Another way of crafting your why is to look at what the benefits of working with you or the service you offer are. Answer the same question over and over! It feels a bit daft but honestly this is a really good tactic for any of the big questions that need answering as it gets into the inner workings of your brain. Below is an example of a series of questions a business that sells dog food may take:

Proposed purpose: We sell high-quality dog food.

Why is that important? Dog food provides optimal nutrition for dogs.

And why is that important? Dogs become healthier and more energetic.

And why is that important? Healthier, more energetic dogs have a better quality of life.

And why is that important? Dogs can live longer, happier lives with their owners.

And why is that important? Owners experience more joy and less stress from having healthy, happy dogs.

Committing to your why inspires and motivates everyone involved, and even if that is just you for now in your team then it's a bloody good place to start anyway. It helps you prioritise what really matters, clarifies what you want to achieve and gives you a clear direction to follow, a bit like a north star guiding your way.

This is a bit like dog training where you need to put some effort in to see any result. However, do not overthink it, keep it simple. Time should absolutely be dedicated to thinking about your why and, more importantly, writing all your notes and thoughts down. But do not spend weeks and months doing this. Set aside a day or two to work on the first section of this book with no dog appointments booked in! We know it's really hard to think of turning work away but this is a good habit to start creating. Dedicate time to doing this. It will absolutely pay off in the long term.

By now you've hopefully got a story running through your head. You can see your story as clear as day and you've started thinking about why you do what you do. It is worth noting that neither of us had done any of this work in our businesses in those early years, and arguably it did not stop us from making money to live and feel like we had made it in this self-employed gig of life. However, when we look back now, it was winging it on every single level. Long hours, no clarity on anything we were doing, no sales process, not even sure what we were actually delivering. We just kept creating services to sell to bring in some money. We literally just pitched ourselves as dog trainers and hoped for the best!

Those two businesses generated between £18,000 to £25,000 each year and we'd tell ourselves, "Check us out! That's someone else's full time salary and I'm able to do this by working with dogs which is something I love!" Yet we all know what comes off the back of that: long working hours, emotional drainage and panic every month about where the next pay cheque is coming from. However, when we did the work that we're now outlining for you in this book and we got "business serious," our earnings multiplied by nearly 10 times, with an increase of £90,000+ within a 10-month period, on top of what we had previously been generating.

We also remember thinking at the time of doing this work, "How on earth is identifying my why and purpose supposed to help me increase revenue? Surely I should be working on lead generation strategies to get more enquiries in because I have a service and I just need to sell more of it!" We hear you and 100% get it. But trust this process, it has worked for us and continues to work for our clients who are now increasing their profits in their businesses, gaining time back to enjoy life and actually helping more people and their dogs, which is surely what it's all about.

This piece of work works for thousands of companies outside of the dog-training industry around the globe also. In this industry, we tend to be quite insular and not look any further afield, staying within the confines of the dog industry and looking to other dog businesses for support. We seek advice from other dog businesses going through the same thing, which acts as a self-fulfilling prophecy of our own thoughts that it's a really difficult industry to thrive in because this is what people who are on the same level as you will say. It doesn't make logical sense when you think about it, seeking advice from companies doing the exact same as you, rather than looking to companies that are where you want to be.

So let's jump back into the importance of your why and how this is going to help you grow your business. Let's assume for now that you do know your why. For example, our why for creating Canine Business Academy is to elevate the dog-training profession by fostering a collaborative and professional community where dog-specific entrepreneurs are recognised for their high standards of quality. We aim to create a movement of unity and support, providing trainers with the tools, knowledge and support systems needed to build profitable, value-driven businesses they love and that love them back.

Can you see the determination in that? When we repeat our why it lifts us up and drives determination and motivation to get shit done and pioneer a change. When we get stuck for ideas or when we're looking to see who we can interview next on the podcast or who is going to be best to support our free and paid training, we go back to this and it helps us identify people who align with this view and can help push this message further.

What's yours?

Chapter 4
Core Business Principles

Now that we have our why firmly planted in our minds, we need to get a bit more 'business official' which essentially means putting your why into action. The reason behind doing this is so that it creates a culture that you, your staff (whether you have any or not) and your clients can live in. Every company exists within a realm of trust with people around them. It doesn't matter in the first instance what the product is, as long as there is trust. Putting your why into these next steps helps you bring them to life and will externally exude a thought process that this company – your company – can be trusted.

Steps Toward Cementing Your Why

1. **Create a Set of Company Core Values**

Firstly, what is a core value? They are defined as "beliefs and principles that you believe are important in the way that you live and work. They determine your priorities, guide your decisions and guide the way you act towards others." [3]

Values of the business could be seen as what guides all decisions. For example, one of our values for Canine Business Academy is that we collaborate and connect. By having this as one of our core values it allows us to drive the business forward by ensuring we're speaking with as many people as possible. It also allows us to question any decisions that come up to see whether or not the other person or business we're connecting with shares that same value. And if they don't, it's a red flag to us to say we probably wouldn't work well together. Another one of our values is that we bring fun and energy, which means we have to check in with ourselves when we're showing up externally to ensure we're living this value to bring fun to anyone who is around us.

It is worth noting here that ideally you will have two sets of values. A personal set, which is how you operate in your life with things that are important to you and a company set, which is how the company operates. Even if you are doing this gig by yourself, the business often has separate values to what your personal ones are. You never know where your business will take you and even if you are adamant that it's only going to be you forever, you honestly never know. We can 100% relate to this.

Our advice is to keep the business and yourself separate. It will serve you well by creating some distance between the two. Company values will align with the business' why and help you create purpose and a sense of commitment. They are values that will guide you in making decisions on how to move your business forward. They help identify whether or not a person is a good fit to work with both in client terms, staff and who you're investing your time and money in, i.e. a mentor or peer group. When thinking about tactics such as marketing, your values will help you create content ensuring your messaging has clarity and purpose. Your business and personal values may cross over at times because they may be guided by you in the first instance.

Vicky had no business values in her old dog-training business and realised she was working in a way that didn't align with her personal values. Running puppy classes on a slippery village hall floor for years was what she had been taught was the right way to do things. It was drummed into her that classes shouldn't be done outdoors as everyone will get too cold and the conditions may not be conducive to learning. This didn't really take into consideration the lack of space between one another, or the potential health implications of the slippery floors on young developing dogs. For years, Vicky trusted in the belief that classes were only to be offered in warm, indoor surroundings which ultimately led to a fixed mindset approach of "This is just how it is" despite her gut saying otherwise. If you too have an internal passion such as this, one of your business values may be something like: "We always consider the dogs' needs" or "Dogs are always at the heart of everything we do."

Here's a great example of values within a company outside of the dog training arena.

Google has their values set as "Ten things we know to be true" [4]:

- Focus on the user and all else will follow.
- It's best to do one thing really, really well.
- Fast is better than slow.
- Democracy on the web works.
- You don't need to be at your desk to need an answer.

- You can make money without doing evil.
- There's always more information out there.
- The need for information crosses all borders.
- You can be serious without a suit.
- Great just isn't good enough.

One way you can see Google using their values as a guide to support their products and service is on their search page. Google's search page is clean and clear with no adverts, no access to email, just a search bar because it is important for the customer experience. Google identified that having all the "stuff" on their search page actually made search times slower. When they were removed, the experience sped up and got you to the information faster. This was all driven by their value set.

Creating and knowing your values is important, no matter where you are on the journey.

Maybe you are just starting out, maybe you're a training veteran and have been doing it a long time. You may have zero aspiration to ever have a team. You may want to purely be online only and venture into the passive income space. You might be overjoyed if you can consistently earn £30,000 to £50,000 each year doing the hours you want to do. You may want to have a six-figure business and even a multi-six-figure business. Doing these exercises are crucial for any type of business you want to have, not just the big go-getter types. Even if you simply want to have it as a hobby and side hustle and create £5,000 per annum, this step is important. You ideally want a list of around five to six. Although as you've seen from the example provided above, the number doesn't really matter as long as the principles of you being able to remember them and more importantly, being able to live and breathe them, are there.

Here's how you can start to think about values and how to go about creating a set. First, think of values that are important to you. "We collaborate and connect" is a tenet Canine Business Academy was created on, so that absolutely had to be one of our values. Think of things that are going to help guide your decisions you make in your business. Keep it short. Ideally you'd like to be able to remember them and for them to be easy to understand.

After setting your values, set goals. Your decisions will impact the outside world and also the internal culture for any employees, including yourself. Think about how you want your company to interact with your clients and be seen by others in the industry. Be specific. No jargon.

Lastly and most importantly, be unique. No one else is you. Be totally unapologetically yourself and create values that truly resonate with your business (also another of our values!). If you copy others and become generic, you will not stand out. It will be difficult to base anything else off your values because they do not inspire you and therefore, will not inspire anybody else.

It may feel alien to do this exercise and the first ones you jot down may feel like utter shite, but keep going until you land on ones that light you up a little and make you feel determined to keep going.

2. Create Your Mission (Statement)

A mission statement takes your why and crafts it in a simple guiding statement that anyone both internally and externally will be able to read and have an immediate understanding of what your business is all about. Having a mission statement elevates you as a serious business. It focuses on the daily habits of the business and how you strive to focus on your overall mission.

The first time we heard about this we thought our faces said it all. Huh?!

Simon Sinek, who wrote *Start With Why: How Great Leaders Inspire Everyone to Take Action*, explains that "People don't buy what you do, they buy why you do it." This is a really powerful concept and one that from experience, we've seen people struggle with. It's really challenging when your mindset is that your customers do not care about this and just want their dog "fixed" – whether that's a problem behaviour solved, a groom or a vet check. We can assure you that you need to spend time on resolving this thought process because a limiting mindset will impact your ability to tackle these steps to have a positive outcome on your business.

This is where we go back to your why. We now need to articulate in a brief description what the purpose of your business is to the outside world and how it will serve your potential clients through the type of service you offer.

You can weave in your values and business ethics if they work well together. The mission statement is designed to detail your cause and for people, both actual customers and potential customers, to see in a snapshot exactly what you're about and whether or not they can relate to you.

Below are two examples of mission statements that help you really identify with the company. A good mission statement is one that you can keep going back to every time a decision needs to be made. Every stem has to align with the mission and what the business is trying to achieve.

Some examples of good mission statements[5]:

> Pupnaps: To help your beloved fur-babies have the greatest sleep possible.

> Starbucks: With every cup, with every conversation, with every community – we nurture limitless possibilities of human connection.

How to start crafting your mission statement:

- **Be brief.**
  Think about where this could be used. You don't want reams of words taking over any marketing materials.
- **Be you.**
  What makes you, you? No one else is you. Others may offer the same services as you, but they are not you. What highlights you? Don't copy

someone else, be unapologetically you and that will be memorable for all the right reasons.

- **Know your audience.**
  Who do you want to attract? Your mission statement is aimed at resonating with the people you want to buy your services.

- **Create expectations.**
  What can your customers expect from working with you?

- **Be realistic.**
  This is a hard one! It's easy to want to take over the world but make sure that you are going to be able to achieve your mission.

- **Be positive.**
  People buy happiness and not doom and gloom. Inject positivity and it will give you an energy boost as well.

- **Treat it as a guide.**
  Your statement acts like the end destination on a map. It helps decide the routes you're going to take to get there.

Vicky's mission statement for her old dog-training business before merging with Jo's was "Cheerleading a new movement in canine behaviour and health."

Simple, to the point and incorporated both main aspects of her business. Of course it can be longer, but sticking to the tips above will help to keep you focused.

It can be easy to feel overwhelmed with this work, especially when you've never done anything like this before. Our advice is not to overthink it. Follow the steps above and you'll land on something that works well for you. Then if you end up wanting to change it as you continue to grow and learn, it's your business – you totally can.

3. Create Your Vision

This is where you get to dream big! Use your why to truly inspire a vision for your business and have fun with ideas on what you could achieve if you knew how to get there. An end goal is always the best place to start so you can backtrack the steps on how to get there. The fancy term is reverse engineering.

The vision statement is designed to get you feeling excited and keep you moving in the right direction. When everything starts aligning, studies prove that companies grow revenue 58% faster and are 72% more profitable.[6]

When we decided to embark on our journey of creating Canine Business Academy back in 2023, we had a loose idea of what it was we were wanting to do. The rough idea was that we felt that dog trainers need the knowledge that we have on how to implement business and that this could be offered in some form of coaching.

We met up most weeks at a little farm shop restaurant where we consumed poached egg on toast with baked beans in a vessel, alongside copious amounts of tea and cake (the latter was mainly Jo). Laptops were in tow and outsiders looking in on these "meetings" might have been thinking "Oh, this looks a bit fancy and clearly they know what they're doing." We did not.

We had this great idea and so much knowledge but just couldn't seem to get anything to align. With knowledge comes a big disadvantage. Sometimes, because we think we know all the things that we need or, should we say, want, to be doing, we end up thinking we can skip over the steps of business basics. So that's exactly what we did!

We ended up crafting a product we called MentorMind because at the time we had a few people asking us how to be dog trainers. We saw a need out there for journeys to be crafted to allow for shadowing, hands-on real life experience alongside theory knowledge as well. So we dabbled in this space. We pulled a programme together and sold two spaces immediately.

This was a really good learning curve for us because whilst the programme was a success, it was not the vision we had for Canine Business Academy. In fact, at that time, we were actually called Rebel Core Collective! We thought we wanted to be rebellious and have a tribe of people we could refer to as rebels.

Again, this was an epic failure because no one knew what the hell Rebel Core Collective was. All the values, mission and vision were not clear, certainly not to us, so 100% not to anyone else out there. We look back on this now and laugh because we know all of this stuff yet did not apply it! What utter twats.

Six months were spent dicking around with what we acronymed RCC and all that time, we could not for the life of us figure out what the hell we were doing. We were both disheartened because there was a short period of time where we excused ourselves as being busy in our dog-training businesses and did not spend much time together in that farm shop. However, in early December 2023 we had a lightbulb moment. We sat down and did this work with a new lease of life in us because our why was just too strong to ignore. We invested in ourselves on a strategy day, a conference and an additional two courses to help propel our ideas forward. One of those courses did end up being a waste of time, although arguably it also helped us realise what we didn't want either so both turned out to be good investments for different reasons.

Fast forward and Rebel Core Collective evolved into Canine Business Academy. We launched with a Number 1 podcast, with over 22,000 downloads in the first 12 weeks and a business that generated £40,000 in sales within that same 12-week period. All this was achieved because we had clear values, a mission and a vision for the future of this business, all of which led to creating an implementable strategy that helped us achieve these goals.

Picture where you want your business to be in five or ten years. Think about your ultimate success and don't be afraid to dream big. This is what your vision statement is all about. It outlines your dream for the future of your business. Just note that this is not the right place to include a detailed plan of how to get there.

Here are some examples of good vision statements[7]:

> BBC: To be the most creative organisation in the world.

> Disney: To make people happy.

> Google: To provide access to the world's information in one click.

Here are some questions to help you define your vision: Where do you want the business to be headed? What can you realistically achieve? What problem do you want to solve? How can your business make a difference for individuals and the industry? What will change if your vision becomes reality? What words describe the outcome you desire?

Keep your vision specific to your business. It's essential to be bold and even take risks when crafting your vision statement.

Your vision statement ideally needs to be brief and straightforward. Avoid being overly detailed. Focus on one or two key points that convey a clear vision. Stay away from jargon terms and use the present tense.

Aim for clarity rather than trying to make it catchy. A great vision statement is simple, memorable and inspirational.

The most important thing we want you to take away from this part is to have fun and dream big dreams. You can absolutely have the business that you want in whatever way that looks like for you. You may want to be the best known local trainer in your area for a particular outcome and that's an amazing vision to aspire to. You may want to go bigger and make huge changes in the industry. It's your dream, your vision and something you could have a lot of fun creating.

4. Create Goals

Now that we have a clear idea of our values, mission and vision, we can craft goals to help achieve them. Some goals may not be a direct link to your mission and vision, such as reaching a certain financial target, but all goals are important to write down so that we can create a strategy behind each of them to help us achieve them.

Goals are a way of helping you measure success in any way you define it. They help other members of staff (if you have any) see what you're trying to do and help keep everyone motivated to move forward. For example, when we decided to write this book, we set ourselves the goal to have it published within an eight-month period for a particular event we knew we needed to be at. We then realised, through the help of our publisher, that meant writing the whole thing within an eight-week period! But we did it! It was tough but without that goal, well you wouldn't be reading this now.

This admittedly was quite a mountainous goal, but yours can be as big or as small as you want as long as they are achievable and are crafted specifically for you so as not to cause you to be overwhelmed. Your business goals also need to be based on the strategy part we covered earlier. There is zero point creating goals that bear no relation or have no contribution to the overall plan or success of the business.

When we decided to start the podcast and were deliberating the investment of the agency and editing or production fees, the goal of what we wanted to achieve by creating a podcast came into play. We could have absolutely started doing it by ourselves. The three-day podcast course we undertook gave us all of the tools and information to be able to go out there, purchase all the necessary equipment and DIY the lot.

Did we feel that this was sustainable short-term? Absolutely.

Did we want to do this part? Absolutely not.

Did we feel that this was sustainable long-term when all the other demands of a business kicks in? Not a chance.

We knew we didn't want the podcast to be a flash in the pan and only around for a few months until the busyness of life inevitably took over. We also knew we wanted weekly episodes and for this to be consistently posted on the same day each week which added in additional work. All things considered, the agency investment for us, although substantial, was a no-brainer and its value was significant. Ultimately, the goal of serving others and continuing to spread our message globally to be able to maintain momentum in shifting the attitude of our industry relied on whether we made the investment as far as we were concerned.

Now, think about some goals that will drive *you* forward and make a list.

Would you like more free time? A bigger house? The ability to travel more? All of these are personal goals that drive you, but have nothing to do with where you want to get your business. Your business goals will, however, impact your ability to achieve your bigger purpose with your personal goals being a product of reaching them.

Start off by doing a dump of what's in your head on goals you'd like to achieve. Don't worry about separating them into business and personal at this stage if that feels like too much. It's just a really good place to start to get everything written down. Once you have them in front of you, some of them may come as a shock for a couple of different reasons. Some of those goals may have seemingly come from nowhere and you're not quite sure why they came out. Some of them you may be looking at and thinking they're either far too ambitious and you may not believe deep down that you could achieve them. Or on the other hand, you might feel you've played it too safe. The more you do exercises like these, the more you get to know about yourself.

Once you've got some goals down in front of you, add a time frame to each one. For example, if you want to have more time to spend with family, then be super clear with how you'll achieve that. This goal could look like this: "From this date, I will only work one evening every week and one weekend per month." You've now got a time frame to implement some changes and now know what you're working towards. Try to be realistic here otherwise it will not feel achievable and it may put you off thinking any of this is possible. So using this example of more time back, you could say you want to achieve that goal within a three-month period. This allows you to really look at things you can implement within a time frame that is realistic and achievable.

Have a go at separating them into business and personal goals. For example, a personal goal could be to pay yourself a salary of £50,000 by a certain date, so in order to achieve that, the business goal might need to be turning over a revenue of £80,000+ within the same time frame (the figures will change depending on expenses and outgoings). This helps you see what then needs to be done to help achieve these figures and gives you a realistic thought process of how many of your current services you would need to sell in order to achieve that goal.

Have fun with this! This is where you get to dream big and you might start to look at your business with a bit more enthusiasm than you may have done previously.

Trust the process. This is just the start.

Chapter 5
The Story of You

Every successful business has a story behind it, a journey that explains how it came to be. Your origin story is the essence of your brand, capturing the experiences, motivations and values that have shaped who you are today. Think of it as the narrative that not only defines who you are but also connects you deeply with your customers.

An engaging origin story does more than just chronicle your past; it helps establish your brand's identity and builds a bridge of trust and emotional connection with your audience. Just like how Apple's garage beginnings or Nike's athlete-driven innovation resonate with millions, your story can make a lasting impression and set you apart from others, leaving you in a great position to do what you do best.

When we both started our respective dog-training businesses, it's fair to say they started in a similar way to most: We had no clue, loved dogs and just started doing and copying what others were doing. We think you get the gist by now. It's an interesting journey when you go back over these business basics because it's the work you never really think about at the time of doing anything in your business or life. Reflection is a practice we could all implement more often.

If you're anything like Jo though, this is the hardest part because it doesn't feel like doing this is going to move the needle any further forward on achieving your goals. She is definitely the one-half of this duo who is very goal-driven. For Jo, having a massive to-do list that can be created and smashed through is doing something productive; the intangible actions completed to bring money into the business or propel the business forward isn't. Depending on your personality, you may also fall into this camp, or you could be the complete opposite and much prefer doing what Jo refers to as the "fluffy" stuff because the other tactics feel out of line with your heart-centred approach around dogs. Neither is right or wrong, but it's having self-awareness of how you feel about things and then finding ways to help you get into the mindset of completing these tasks.

Business is a funny game because whether we like it or not, the key driver to any business is making money. Without it, it's not really a business and more of a glorified hobby. For a lot of us dog professionals out there, it's a real challenge to see yourself as a separate entity to the business because you're the one doing everything. It's really common for you to think you are the business. This is an important reminder again that you are not the business. You run, own, work in the business, but the business is not you. What is important is making sure your business has a founder's story and tying this in with how you came about creating your mission and vision, so that potential clients can relate to your business.

By spending time understanding your story, you unlock a wealth of knowledge about yourself that you may not have even realised, because it's not a task any of us really do. Not only can this help with building solid foundations for your business, you can also weave your story into your marketing because people love and connect with stories. Think about it. Take a moment to reflect over your life.

Can you see any reason as to why you ended up working with dogs? Sometimes it feels as though you've just landed on this trajectory and your past has nothing to do with it. That may be the case, but there will be moments in your life that have helped shape you into the person you are today, the same person that created your dog business.

If you don't fully immerse yourself in knowing who you are, you will continually tell yourself stories that potentially aren't true. Everything you have experienced has created the person you are today. This person makes all the decisions for the business, how you view clients, how you view your pricing structure, why you may or may not want a team and why you want to work the hours you do and the type of tasks that you do. By simply saying things like, "Well, this is just who I am," you are doing everyone around you a disservice because you become unrelatable. This is why it is important to understand it because you get to learn a lot about yourself which can positively impact your business.

When Vicky tackled this task, this is what she realised: Shyness had affected her from a young age and held her back in various ways during her childhood. Her ability to enjoy her early days at school, the ability to make friends easily and the opportunity to enjoy experiences that she had at times felt too worried about participating in, were all outward symptoms of her lack of confidence. That early experience she had at the pub job transformed how she felt about herself. It was the beginning of a whole new chapter that allowed her to flourish, become open and willing to learn new things, as well as take on the responsibility that enabled growth and confidence in her own skills.

Try this exercise: Write down any and all moments in your life, not just specific to your business and have a look to see where you can see any patterns, or if certain experiences or connections keep popping up in your life. See if you can identify any theme. Lean into personal challenges, triumphs and experiences, think about anything you've done that has made you feel a great sense of accomplishment.

Ask yourself the following questions: What skills did you learn during that experience? How have you applied that skillset and learning to other endeavours in your life? Look at your professional trajectory, how did you come about choosing the path you've done previously? Was it family influences? Was it an inner thing driving you? How and why did you choose the jobs you have done?

It's easy sometimes to think that you just fell into it or it was a case of just getting a job to get some money. But we're quite complex as human beings. There will be a pattern that emerges in all of your decisions and they have been crafted by experience, learnings and sometimes a bit of what's in us. But hey, we're preaching to dog experts here! We know this is the case for dogs, but do we bring it to the forefront of our minds that we are on similar paths?

What were your passions and interests in childhood? If you didn't have a family dog in childhood, what else were you doing? Jo didn't grow up with any pets. What she remembers is spending days playing and biking with her sister and other kids on the street she grew up on. They played games like Acky Acky 123 and a bit of cricket – or rounders – stopping only for the one or two cars that would pass by the whole day! How do these interests show up in your life today? In Jo's case, the feeling of connectedness and the joy that comes from simplicity absolutely shows up in her business life today and how she connects with clients. Being able to simplify what may seem like complicated training or behaviour techniques when speaking with clients is a skill in itself and could be linked back to these memories and experiences. Perhaps you can't see the connection yet. This work is pretty deep and you can see why you could procrastinate over it because who on earth has the time to do all this stuff? You might feel like you need a week sitting by a pool or a beach to do this reflective work but alas the turbulent weather of the UK calls so your office will have to suffice for now. In all seriousness, you don't actually need to dedicate a whole week to doing this work, but you do need to dedicate *some* time to this.

Your story will start coming together and you'll become more articulate, a skill you need to be able to help customers see what they are truly signing up for when they decide to work with you. Because although, yes, they are essentially wanting a problem resolved, people buy from people. And the more your story resonates with someone, then the likelier they'll want to buy from you and stay with you.

Think about all the relationships you've had with people in your life. Who have been the people who influence you and support you? Are they the same person? Are they different? What made you choose that person when thinking about an influencer for you? What did you connect with?

Since embracing her personal development and business journey a few years ago, Vicky has been a huge fan girl of someone who is quite "famous" in the business world and was literally obsessed with everything this person put out. She just had to buy all the stuff. They could literally put anything out and she'd want to buy it just because of who it was putting the products out there. Jo was aware of this person but didn't have the same feeling of awe about them and essentially disregarded a lot of stuff as just another person in the space who's doing well but *meh*. She could take or leave it.

But when Jo finally saw this person at a conference in person, she changed her mind. Sure, she paid a bit more attention than normal because of Vicky's obsession, but that wasn't it. It was this person's story of why she created her business. Jo really resonated with her story. She felt even more inspired after learning that this person achieved success while raising two young children, had no support from family (who all thought she was crazy for her career choices), was a totally busy person who was taking on so much because she could see her goals so clearly. These were all things that Jo was experiencing too. The point being, without that story Jo wouldn't have switched over to the other side of the fence. Now we both know her content is amazing and 100% cannot be argued with! She knows her stuff! But there was no connection until the story was heard. Now if the story didn't resonate then that's totally fine, it wouldn't have affected us or how we do anything as such, but it did affect this person's business because she gained a new client: Jo.

This task could potentially seem difficult if you're unsure whether your story has any value to what it is you're offering. It might also be difficult if you are quite a private person and potentially you may be hardwired to only give information which is more about facts rather than your value. The upside to creating a story about how you've come to run this business and linking it with your mission and vision is so that people can connect with you and understand the business more. It allows you to stand out and be memorable in a sea of the same. As you grow, you may want to go all in on a marketing strategy around your story and how your story can impact others positively. This can be used for a lot of content across various platforms and for when you're speaking about your business to prospective partnerships or clients.

Once you've done some of the personal work to learn more about yourself, it's time to turn your attention to the business and do a similar exercise. For this, think about the why of your business again and use this as a starting point.

Here's an example snippet of how an origin story can show up in your business: "After a tough childhood spent in social housing, Lisa went on to have successful careers in law, banking and the entertainment industry. Her background in overcoming obstacles has helped mould her into a bold, straight-talking coach who is never afraid to be an authentic and outspoken truth-teller."

This story will do one of two things, it will either attract people who like the sound of her, or it will put them off – which does this business a favour because then they're not having to speak with a client that is never going to buy from them.

Use the following template to help:

The Why of Your Business

I started my business because …

The lightbulb moment that caused me to create the business was ...

What's the Story Behind My Story?
Looking back at my personal experiences, thoughts and feelings, I can now see...

I recognise there is deep value in these events because...

This has made me realise that what I do now is so important because...

It's possible that the general public see all dog trainers as much of a muchness, because the services and offerings tend to be pretty similar across the board. This potentially explains why you might feel that the only differentiating factor between you and the next dog trainer down the road is price. We encourage you to think about how potential clients could start to see the value in you and your business and how this sets you apart instead.

Creating your origin story is a strategic asset for your business. Remember, an engaging story creates trust, builds emotional connections and ultimately influences customer loyalty and decision-making. As you go on this journey, integrate your story into your marketing efforts, from your website and social media to client interactions. This isn't just about attracting customers, it's about creating a meaningful and lasting impact. Your story not only defines you but also inspires others. You are sitting on a mountain of value just in the story of yourself. If you start telling your story, you'll be amazed at what happens next.

Chapter 6
Your Niche, Your Genius

Focus on one thing. Do it well repeatedly. Become an expert.

It really is that simple. So why do we over complicate it?

When you hear the word "niche," what do you think? In our experience we've found that being niche scares a lot of people because it's misunderstood and the thought process might be that it limits the amount you can earn or deliver. You only have to look at any dog trainers website to identify this is a real thing.

Let's try looking at a niche with a growth mindset and how this could absolutely be the platform to you creating consistent income, becoming an expert and going all in on something you love! Think about some of the different brands you buy from and know. One that jumps to mind immediately is The Muzzle Movement. They've gone all in on their messaging and products with muzzles. They weren't trying to be everything to everyone, yet now have a very large consumer market with a lot of hype around them at the time of writing this book in 2024. They've diversified into leads and collars amongst other things as they've grown but the name hasn't changed and what they're known for hasn't changed. They got really really good at one thing, repeated it and became known for it.

One of the reasons you may be feeling this way is that as trainers, we have a collective habit of spreading ourselves too thinly, constantly seeking validation from our peers, and finding ourselves always on the lookout for that next shiny CPD badge to help with that much needed dollop of confidence boosting. If we just got good, and we mean really sh*t hot, at the *one thing* we love doing and feel mega passionate about, imposter syndrome would be kicked to the curb in an instant.

When Vicky first became a dog trainer in 2007, her biggest fear was that she was going to struggle to be seen and stand out amongst all the other trainers in her area doing similar things.

We've already alluded to additional services being added so pop yourself in the mindset of Vicky for a moment.

Vicky started her training journey with an organisation who prided themselves in giving newbies just like her all of the tools to become an amazing puppy trainer. She was attracted to the company values that would, she hoped, help set her apart from others running puppy classes in the local area.

Becoming a qualified puppy trainer (as well as receiving a shiny new certificate and a listing on the website, ding! Winner!) in her eyes was an amazing opportunity to create a fantastic niche business and push it out into the market, which at the time, there was a huge gap for. Just imagine being *the* go-to expert in your field for all things puppy! She was so excited to embark on this journey, and having previously worked for one of the largest UK animal rehoming charities for the four years prior, had seen the irreparable damage a lack of socialising and training a puppy at a young age could do.

Encouraging anyone with a brand new puppy to put the work in early enough to avoid the chances of them being relinquished into rescue was the driving force behind her mission to do better for dogs.

As an ambassador for the puppy organisation, there were a set of values and stipulations that needed to be adhered to:

- Puppies attending would all be 20 weeks and under.
- All family members were encouraged to attend classes for consistency.
- A fun and friendly ethos containing a syllabus of life skills suitable for everyday scenarios.
- Classes were designed to be progressive, meaning skills were gradually built on week-by-week.
- An upper class size limit of eight puppies.

On the whole there were lots of positives and this all sounded very different from what most other trainers were offering locally. In addition, there was the promise of the opportunity to become part of a supportive network of peers to share ideas, problems and wins with. Wow! If you are reading this as a practising dog trainer, we are pretty sure you know that this is something fundamentally lacking within our little world.

Meetups, conferences, a forum (and we're talking pre-Facebook – this was the retro email type back in the mid-noughties for anyone else who can remember) were all provided, and aided our ability to connect regularly with the comfort of knowing that we were not alone in going through similar struggles and challenges within our businesses. In theory, all of this did set this organisation apart from most others at the time and was hands-down by a mile, the best part. It really was a niche going all in on puppies!

The way the organisation constructed itself had every ethos about puppies. They weren't trying to be anything else and there was zero chance of any confusion about what you were going to get. Every word, every message exuded puppies.

There was so much potential for Vicky to create an amazing niche and fulfil her dream of being the expert in puppy training in her local area, but the fear crept in. The fear of turning other work down and of being *too* niche took over.

Having left that organisation and having the freedom to do what she wanted actually didn't serve her very well, as the thought of being "just" a puppy trainer suddenly no longer felt enough. Of course this resulted in the addition of a plethora of services: follow-on puppy class; adolescence class; short courses and workshops for recall, loose lead, reactivity; dog sports including agility and hoopers, scentwork; and even dog yoga.

Oh, and not to mention topping up her income with dog walking and the odd 1:1 training session. It's actually exhausting listing them all out and thinking about it all!

The thought of focusing on just one thing and niching down may well be scaring the hell out of you right now. You may also have a few other questions whirring around your head as well including:

What about all of the potential clients I would be turning away?

Won't I lose potential income?

What if there isn't a lot of that specific type of dog in my area? I also live in a rural area so shouldn't I take all that I can get?

Won't clients end up going to the other trainer down the road who does or uses XYZ instead?

Just like you, we battled with most of these thoughts at some point. Get this, though. If your product stands out by tackling a very specific struggle experienced by many, it will sell.

Being too generalised means you may be lost in a crowd of others doing very similar things, which only leaves price as a comparable. Can you see how this is currently playing out everywhere you look? In every area, there are new dog trainers popping up every week. The fear of dealing with this is real for many.

The fear of business being taken away and the worry of not being good enough both result in leading your business by price. Prospective clients may find it difficult to differentiate one from another, which means they are likely to enquire with many and potentially go with the first person that comes back to them because there's not much else to go on.

Another way to look at this is through a customer's viewpoint. Put yourself in a customer position for just a moment. Imagine you are now wanting to invest in some marketing and you've decided that social media is going to be the focus.

There are several people offering marketing services across all the different platforms at such a choice that you have no idea where to start. You then come across someone who refers to themselves as a Facebook ads expert which gets you thinking about dialling in on one specific platform. You then find someone else who states they're a pet business Facebook ads expert. Already you may feel more of a pull to the second one because you may believe they understand your industry more and what you're hoping to achieve. If there was one further that said dog training Facebook ads expert then you might be likely to think you'd be on to a winner (assuming you're a dog trainer).

Niching down doesn't always have to mean you only serve one breed of dog or dog issue. The type of offer you create, and perceived value you deliver can also be niche. We will talk about crafting a compelling offer for your clients in the next chapter, but for now, we are here to remind you that *you* can do whatever *you* want to do within your business. Positioning yourself as an expert doesn't at all refer to being big headed. It also doesn't have to be scary, or mean that you need to pretend to know things you have no real clue about.

If you're reading this and find yourself doubting the importance of positioning yourself as an expert, consider these three points.

Why would someone choose to work with you over the next person? If the same services are being offered, what differentiates you from another?

What have you got to lose? And what have you got to gain? On average, dog trainers earn £15,000 to £18,000 per year with traditional offerings. Thinking outside the box and implementing new ways of working, such as those suggested in this book, could help you achieve better outcomes for clients, as well as more time, freedom and profitability for you too. Are you gunning for £40,000, £60,000, or £80,000? Whatever your financial goal, they are all possible!

You can always change and become more general as you grow!

Try not to focus too much on what others are doing and instead focus on where your passion lies. This is where you can refer back to your why, your values, and your overall vision for the business. We actively encourage you to think outside the box when it comes to the norm. Oh, and our favourite? Ditch conformity! We are especially partial to this one, as anyone who knows us will testify to. Our industry has a bizarre and intrinsic need to split all of its services and offer them out in a bitty mix-and-match model. We have no idea where this originally came from to be perfectly honest, but it certainly does not lend itself to being niche. It just creates more of what everyone else is doing.

Standing your own ground and carving your own path will create stability, grow your passion and develop you and your clients in a way that you never dreamed possible. Suddenly, you'll have clarity on how to craft your messaging and know what to say on social media because you have a thing that you can talk about and go all in on. You will be able to immediately identify whether or not a client is good for you or whether they would be better served by someone else. You will be able to operate from a place of service as you're able to go all in on your expertise and deliver something magical. You absolutely don't have to do this, and you absolutely don't have to be reading this book. But you are, which suggests you could be that person that is willing to buck the trend this industry has created and go all in on creating an expert space for people to buy into and refer on to.

We've already mentioned The Muzzle Movement, but look at others including Michael Shikashio with Aggressive Dog, Kim Brophey with ethological views on dogs and Kids Around Dogs which pretty much does what it says on the tin. Without these niches, where are you likely to go to find out more about these particular areas?

Great! But how do you figure out what you can become an expert *at* or *in*? Make a list of what lights you up!

What gets you excited or what do you keep geeking out on?

What training or behaviour issues do you love getting your teeth into and make you want to jump out of bed in the morning?

What are your favourite breeds?

Who is your ideal client? Try creating an avatar!

What is the format that is most conducive to you teaching in, and most receptive for your clients to learn in?

If you struggle with that, try another list of things you also *don't love* about your business, and strip these out. Be ruthless and don't hold back.

Are there certain training or behaviour issues that you don't enjoy or feel confident working with? Reactivity, separation anxiety?

Are there specific breeds that don't float your boat?

Are there certain types of clients that drive you insane? Non-committal, time poor? A lack of interest in science-based learning or geeky stuff?

Is there a format that just doesn't light you up? Group classes, 1:1 training?

Another way to look at niching is choosing to work with a specific type of person or circumstance someone has. What about young professionals, those who live in cities, busy families, those who travel a lot with their dogs, or even live on the move? The possibilities really are endless. Be selective and immerse yourself in all of the things you have a genuine passion for.

A personal mission of ours is for you, and every other dog trainer out there, to learn to love every single aspect of your business.

You should now have a short list and see with more clarity what you want to be doing. You may still feel twitchy at this point and revert back to those earlier questions of doubting whether or not this would be viable. Try sitting with it for a while and revisit your mindset. Are you looking at this from the perspective of a fixed or growth mindset?

If this still feels like an impossible task for you, go back to your why and mission for the business. When we were creating Canine Business Academy, we were scared to go too niche because our thought process was that the dog industry was already niche enough instead of opening up a wider business strategy company.

We launched and targeted dog professionals, all our wording was dog professionals yet the more we drilled down and worked in our space of genius, it became incredibly obvious, like a huge-slap-in-the-face obvious, that our niche is dog trainers!

It is our experience, our knowledge, our true genius, our passion, and by trying to become more generic in thinking we might reach more people by going a smidge broader, we ended up not reaching anyone.

This is important. Do not overlook the power and positive impact niching can have on your business. If you need more evidence, start to look at every company around you and think about how you buy. You will see examples everywhere you turn of those who do it really well and those who are more generic.

There isn't a right or wrong, but you will certainly have a different experience from companies that are more targeted and niche.

Chapter 7
Nailing Your Offer

Having a service, or services, that align with your company mission, vision and values is super important. We mean, it would be a bit weird if we got this far into the book and suddenly this part, the part you're actually going to use to create something to sell and earn an income from, doesn't have anything to do with the work you've done so far.

Creating the service that you're actually going to sell could indeed feel like a really hard thing to do – that is, if you're willing to buck the norm and put the customer ideals first rather than mimicking what has always been done and what certainly feels like an archaic approach in this day and age. When you look at the services that the dog industry offers you'll be hard pressed to find something that we haven't already mentioned such as an array of classes, 1:1s and workshops.

In 2024, the industry knowledge of dog behaviour is continuing to increase and move forward. It even feels like the public is starting to be aware to a small degree of how important this knowledge is to have, as seen when you look at the work being produced that looks more and more at how a dog needs choice, how old-school obedience as a stand alone doesn't cut it anymore, how different techniques can get the best out of dogs in different situations and how dogs can influence human behaviour as well. Body language is a whole category of its own as well now and we've certainly seen that it's gaining awareness with how there are more clients talking to us about it.

So if all the science is supporting new ways of thinking in this arena, then why is the application of how the services are delivered stuck in the 1990s?

There seems to be an unintentional lack in thinking about how humans and dogs are going to benefit best from the knowledge we now have in terms of how we coach and teach dogs. How often do you reflect on the effectiveness of the standard service model you offer?

Have you explored this topic? Have you gathered feedback from your clients or conducted surveys in your area to assess the success of your model? It's okay if you haven't done this work so far. It's something to perhaps start considering as you move forward in your business.

This particular section will draw upon previous topics mentioned as there are several factors that influence the crafting of your offer.

Firstly, you may feel as though what you ought to offer is what people want. You might be telling yourself people are only ringing around and asking for puppy classes, for example. But maybe there's just nothing else available.

The list of current services offered could probably be found on every dog trainer website which, for all intent and purpose, creates a culture of resource guarding when another dog trainer pops up in your area offering the exact same thing (Hint: Because you're doing the same thing). There is currently nothing distinguishing you from anyone else. Ouch.

This is a reminder why your niche and being unapologetically you are really important. From a prospective client point of view they will be subconsciously grasping to find something in your business that makes you stand out to them over your neighbour.

They may be scouring around your messaging to find something they can connect with.

This may be difficult to read, especially when we know you're putting your heart and soul into the delivery of your work. Just know that it's not your enthusiasm that might be questioned, it's the medium in which it's delivered.

Can you imagine if a huge organisation such as Apple never thought outside the box with their customers? Or if they never had a strong why at the heart of everything they do and just did what had always been done? The products they created off the back of the niche and why are all centred around lifestyle and how these can fit in with your everyday life.

Apple is a great example of how they've created products specifically designed to answer their why. There are thousands of other examples, yet interestingly and quite common across all other industries as well, we seem to think we're a bit special and unique because we work with dogs. Except it's really not.

Everything is changing around you and if you're not moving forward with it and thinking outside the box then you will be left behind. Your business may be doing exceedingly well at the moment with the structures mentioned, but can you confidently say that will be the same in five years time? Are you thinking that far ahead?

Creating a compelling offer has to include the service, but it doesn't end there. Your target audience has to see something in you that they really connect with, which ties in with the messaging piece we've just done. They have to believe that your business is the right solution for them and their dog. What if your service was not only aimed at how you can help the dog, but how you can also incorporate the human too?

By this we don't mean solely working hours that only suit the client, but it does mean considering what your target audience is struggling with. What type of support does the human end need from you? What are your expectations of the human because perhaps you're going to be wanting them to put work in outside of your session, ready to review on your next session? If that's the case, what are you putting in place to set them up to succeed with this? How is it being presented?

For example, in our dog-training business That Canine Co, we set out that we want people to receive an education about their dogs. We understood that from a client's point of view being a dog owner is becoming even more confusing every single day with multiple streams of differing information. They are literally looking for someone to speak to and to help guide them through the confusion that lies out there.

We know that people are consuming various sources; they're trawling YouTube, Google, social media platforms, asking people down at the park, those lovely friends and family members who have dogs (or even don't) that will offer all their advice and opinions. It's the equivalent of being a new parent where you seek to obtain information from any and all available sources rather than seeking a professional. It's a bloody mess out there!

Yet still, we think they know what's best for them and we continue to offer the same services that none of us are enamoured with any more. If we start to really think about our potential customers, it's likely that a high percentage of people will have a typical 9-to-5 job, families to look after, friends to see on top of ad hoc engagements. And when you're not a geek about dogs, then they are likely to invest little time in training without the support of you.

There are several ways of looking at how to best serve your clients. For us, specifically in our dog-training business, we set about crafting a long-term working programme with clients who allowed us to really understand both the dog and people elements in depth. We looked at what people were asking for and what they felt was needed, and for us it landed on support.

By knowing your target audience in depth, it means you can consider how they may want to work with you and what exactly they are looking for. If you were potentially trying to target someone who has an incredibly busy life, meaning they struggle to take their dogs out because the times they have available are either incredibly unsociable hours, or those peak times where quite literally everyone seems to be out with their dogs, then put yourself in their shoes.

That way, you could potentially see how a trained-for-you programme may work for this scenario with the odd support session for when the person could soak up any information needed for them. This type of service offering, when fully thought through to align with your mission, vision and niche, allows for the potential ease of selling a programme that offers a genuine solution to someone's problems.

When you start thinking about the person just as much, if potentially not even a little bit more, you start to tap into true connection with your audience. This allows for the potential of follow-on programmes to exist. This is something we in our business have as a natural next step when an initial programme is ending because the thought process is there for someone who may not be ready to go it on their own just yet.

We have found that having one core service spoken about outwardly allows for so much simplicity that clients find it really easy to understand its value and are therefore able to easily buy. This is the great thing about business, the only right way is your way! It's your business and it should feel like a fun game where you get to test out different things and see what works.

That's exactly how we landed on the way we do things with long term programmes. It felt right for what we were seeing happen in the business and then we tested it to see if our audience wanted it. You then tweak again and review. You keep doing this same thing until you land on something that is working really well and sells with ease time and time again whilst getting results.

Become known for delivering an amazing service in your area of genius. Do this one thing. Do it really well. And repeat.

If you're wanting to attempt doing something a little different, firstly you need to collate information on what it is your current client base loves about you and your services. Think back to our niche section here:

What do you think you are known for? Why would people recommend you? Remember, people never recommend just because of the tactical implementation, e.g. you offer so many sessions, it's about the bigger promise and value piece they get from working with you. If you're confident that you can truly solve the problem in your niche and have clear messaging, then go all in on that.

Start to think about how much time you need. What feels like a good amount of time for you? If you look back over the majority of your clients (because there's always going to be anomalies), how long did they need to see any changes and be truly happy with what they were seeing?

Other questions to consider are: How long until the dog starts to change behaviour in your experience? How long until the human half starts to create new habits? How much accountability and ongoing support do you and they feel is needed? Consider the lack of confidence in humans and the inconsistency in training. This is where really getting into the head of your customer will really help. Consider others who are involved with the dog at home or are in that dog's life and what impact they will have on your overall outcome.

Many times we've been part way through working with someone and a new person pops up and only then do you find out that "Bob" is a big part of the dog's life and takes them out all the time.

Then we need to consider what if the "problem" isn't fixed within your proposed amount of time? Is there an opportunity to continue? What does that look like?

With the above answered, now ask yourself what is the best method of delivery and why? What considerations need to be made? This is where you can start to consider the mechanics of your offer.

For example, if you've been able to answer that on average it takes you three 60-minute sessions to see a result for one training exercise and potentially one session to discuss and provide information and then potentially another session as a review, then could all this be put together in a programme where a customer would buy the whole thing as a solution rather than seeing it as a number of sessions?

This way you are coming across as the professional that has a solution someone can purchase in the form of your service offering.

This may feel daunting but it hopefully also feels quite exciting. By implementing everything so far and truly understanding the answers to the above question, you really get to create a service that works perfectly for both the client and yourself. It will allow you to plan and create forecasts of the work coming in depending on how you craft your offer.

If in doubt because you may have a lot of services, start small and look to tweak one if it feels right. You could potentially even look to combine some of the services together so that it offers a better service to your clients and makes the ease of deliverability feel better.

The most important thing is to keep thinking about the customer, both the human aspect as well as the dog, and you can't go far wrong.

Chapter 8
Messaging

Have you ever sat in front of your computer or phone, tried to post something on social media, but the words just don't come? Or have you tried to write an email and stared blankly at the screen? You probably had all those limiting beliefs flooding your brain with thoughts that nobody wants to hear from you: "I hate emails, and now I'm trying to send one out. No one wants to receive emails. Email marketing just doesn't work!"

You might be beating yourself up internally because you have no idea where to start. You feel you "should" do this because someone told you that in order to have a successful business, you need to be present on social media and email.

This highlights the importance of the previous steps of identifying your Why and what the business's mission and vision is. This is also why understanding where your current mindset is and where you want it to be is all so integral to successful business strategy.

Messaging is the whole perception of your business that is seen through your potential customers' eyes. Our concern in this industry is that it feels like we're trying to post information and content to impress our peers rather than an audience of people who need and want your help. It could be that you are worried about putting any messaging out for the fear of what someone else might say.

Content creation and all the things you get wrapped up in as a business owner becomes so complicated when you don't know what your purpose is. You'll see this when you take a quick gander across any business platforms including their website when they're not sure on what the purpose of the business is. The messaging may be disjointed with styles varying wildly across different platforms. There may be an in-depth About You section stating all the tangibles in credentials and experiences, which reads more like a CV, and a huge section on how much they love dogs. Fact is, most customers would assume a dog trainer loves dogs. Why else would they be doing what they do?

So when you make your messaging, choosing to focus on the elements that might be more useful to customers directly such as what help they need, and how they are currently feeling as a result of the struggles they're experiencing, will prove to be more valuable information.

Photos and videos of dogs you've trained and have done well with your guidance are in essence a nice thing to celebrate, but we need to ask if that relates to a prospective client's current struggles. It might be acting to validate that we are capable of delivering the things we say we can, but by talking directly to the human in need of help and using their language, it will make them feel heard. They are more likely to take an interest because the words you use sound like them and you fully understand their needs.

In Canine Business Academy world, the way we speak to our audience connects in such a way that it prompts us to receive messages such as, "It's like you're describing me exactly!" This is the power of getting your messaging right.

Cutting to the chase and putting out content that will immediately resonate with somebody struggling with a particular problem is key to living in today's fast paced world where attention spans, especially online, are extremely limited.

Let's get back to niching for a moment. If you are passionate about seeing the progression in terrier dogs with high prey drive and seeing that channelled amazingly once they learn the skills you're teaching them, potential customers need to understand and get that vibe within seconds of finding you.

What shows your potential clients that you absolutely love helping people to understand how dogs communicate and how to read their body language? Instead of creating a series of body language posts and videos highlighting the clients lack of knowledge, how about helping them to connect the dots by sharing valuable information that your audience will resonate with? Why is body language important to you? Why should someone pay attention to this? What are the ramifications of not understanding this? What can they do to help with this? How did this become something you're passionate about?

Your message could be a movement you are aiming to pioneer and a legacy of change you would like to leave behind. If something like this is the case, start shouting it from the rooftops! Own every single part of it so that it's clear from the outset what you do, who you are and what you believe in. Yes, this may turn a few people away but this is a good thing. You only want to work with people who align with your values and beliefs anyway for the magic to start to happen!

Regardless as to whether or not you've completed the niche work, there is likely to be some element of niche preference in your business.

For example, if you don't work with large breeds of dogs but only mention this once on a small dark corner of your website that can easily be missed, how would both you and a client that made a potential inquiry for their large dog feel about the time they spent doing so? You likely feel a bit deflated because you were never going to be able to support them. Think about the people you follow on social media. Why do you follow them? The first answer we get when this question is asked is that they do amazing content! The videos are professional, all the stuff and all the things making it look next level.

When you dig a little deeper though, because that previous answer was a surface-level answer and absolutely not the reason you follow them, you'll probably start to see that they have something about them that you like. They teach in a certain way and have a bigger message to share with everyone. You absolutely may follow a few people for the surface-level reason, but you may never buy from them or invest much more time in them aside from to have a little nosey at what they're doing and this is because their messaging doesn't land with you. This is a good thing.

To ensure you are attracting the right type of potential customer from the very first point of contact with you, a successful strategy would be to be completely open and transparent by stating who it is you don't want! For example, you could try writing down a guide for clients you want like:

Our training programmes are not for you if:

- you're hoping for a quick fix;

- you're not interested in finding out about the geeky side of dog training; and
- you're only after a session or two.

This might sound like strange advice. You may be thinking that it doesn't make any sense to turn potential clients away; a sale is a sale! However it can absolutely have advantages by filtering *your people* and help avoid difficult situations later on down the line.

You hopefully now have a brief overview of why messaging is important. So what's the next step? The use of storytelling can really help your audience get to know, like and trust you. Start thinking of ways you can relate experiences that happen to you in all aspects of your life and weave in some subtle messaging about what someone will get if they work with you. Sharing some stuff about you and your life that isn't dog-related will help.

This is known as secondary messaging and is very often the reason many people choose to actually work with someone.

Think about your interests and hobbies. Are you a member of a gym or a club? Anything you particularly enjoy doing at weekends you could share something about? Vicky and her husband Gareth have a motorhome and she will often share little snippets of their trips away with friends.

Putting yourself out there might feel vulnerable at first. We totally get it. The fear of judgement is real, but you can't expect your clients to trust and hire you immediately. Do you trust a stranger and make friends instantly? We're guessing no. A brand new relationship takes time to build and nurture.

Concerns we often hear include:

- What will people think?
- People don't care about my life.
- I have nothing exciting to share with people!

Think about a fly-on-the-wall documentary about someone going about their everyday life. How popular are these? How many people love watching celebrities that are down to earth and "normal" just like us? You may connect with someone relatable, or maybe even someone who reminds you of yourself initially. Your interest may not even fully pique in their product or service until later on down the line!

Also, thinking about outcome and results-driven content is going to be a bigger hook for your audience than labouring too much on the semantics of what you will give them and what exactly is involved. We promise you, they do not need to know this yet.

Let's look at an example of someone needing help with their dog. We've broken this down into key sections with an example message which is heavily emphasised so it is easier to understand.

- **The pain points (or the persistent issue or issues that have led somebody to reach out for help)**
  A nine-month old adolescent puppy has begun barking, growling and lunging at unknown dogs out on walks. He is becoming difficult to manage and his owners are now reluctant to take him on walks. They have tried a few techniques but none of them work and they are at a loss of what to do next. They feel helpless.

  Your messaging
  Think about how you can connect and relate with them, an example copy suggestion could be "We love working with young dogs who suddenly seem to have changed overnight and are now behaving

oddly. Remember that time when you were a teenager and everything just felt hard? It's tough! Imagine having no guidance and support network around you at that time. We want to be your dogs' and your support network. It's tough! But it can be easier."

- **Their motivations for seeking help (or the emotional drivers behind the issue or issues)**

  Feeling embarrassed, frustrated and angry with him on walks. The problem is now causing arguments at home as everybody has a different approach of how to manage it. He is getting very strong and the lunging and pulling behaviour is beginning to repeatedly injure the female owner's back. They have even considered rehoming him.

  Your messaging

  Use their language! Pop in embarrassed, frustrated and angry when you're posting or emailing or even on the website; 80% of purchases made are emotionally led. Get into your clients' heads, and say all of the things they are thinking. This allows you to connect the pain points and the motivations together for a stronger pull to your service. You want them to read your message and feel like it is them you are specifically talking to. You have to lean in on this bit heavily in your content. An example copy suggestion: "Are you feeling embarrassed with your dog on a walk? Are they lunging at everything and you're at a loss of what to do?"

- **The considerations (or the decision-making process before purchasing)**
Does the trainer understand the desired outcome? How long will it take? Is the product or service right for them? Will they like the trainer as a person? How easy will it be to understand the techniques being taught? Will it be at a pace they can manage? What is the next logical step to get things started?

Your messaging
This is the tactical bit that helps the brain apply logic to the emotion. This is important, but not as important as understanding the motivations behind seeking help.

All of these points should be considered carefully and covered within your messaging effectively. Reaching your audience on a deeper level will create connections that will immediately set you apart and allow people to truly connect with you.

Vicky was extremely proud of the achievement she had made in obtaining her Level 4 in canine massage and of the organisation she had qualified with. She wanted to sing about it from the rooftops and subsequently plastered her website with all the jargon thinking this would impress future customers. (In true dog industry form, the canine physio and rehab sector doesn't disappoint on the jargon front). Vicky couldn't wait for people to clamber over each other to sign up and get their dogs treated by her newly qualified magic hands. However, there was more tumbleweed from the canine massage page of the website than the long, dusty Californian road she had driven down a couple of years earlier!

She waited... and waited... and waited some more for the bookings to roll in. A few social media posts advertising this brand new service didn't seem to help either and she became increasingly disheartened at the lack of interest.

All of that hard work to get this qualification she felt so passionately about. What a disappointment. All those ungrateful people who were not even willing to help their dogs, what was the point? People just don't care. Vicky couldn't for the life of her figure out what was going wrong so she decided to ask a few people to cast their eye over the website for some feedback.

Jo was actually one of those friends who she asked to have a quick look.

"It all sounds amazing I think, but what does any of it actually mean?" are the words that came from Jo's mouth – words that nobody wants to hear.

"I already know what it is that you do, but even I am confused and clueless from reading this!" The knife cut in just a little bit deeper.

"Huh? Myotherapy...?" It got too much for Vicky to bear. How dare someone belittle all of the time and money she had put into achieving this? Cue all of the defensive comments that started pouring out.

"But it is amazing, and will really help your dog with their chronic pain using complementary therapy, and no need for drugs..." In hindsight, this defensive outpouring probably lasted around a good 10 minutes if not more.

Finally, there was a glint in Jo's eye. "Ahh-haaaaa... pain!" she said with a huge grin on her face, "That's it!"

"That's what?" Vicky replied, just not comprehending the joyful smirk. "So, are the dogs all suffering from pain that need your help?"

"Erm, well yes, chronic pain."

"That's the angle, the pain point (excuse the pun), the relatable word that will hook people in and help them to understand why they can't be without your service! We just need to cut the jargon and use the word "pain" in all of your messaging!"

And so the "Pain Management Programme" was born.

And do you know what? Jo was right! (She usually is). Vicky and her new service became more relatable and easier to understand. She started talking about the outcomes and results that working with her could deliver, not only from the dog, but human perspective too. And most importantly, she started getting clients!

Once you start getting clear on your messaging, put it everywhere. Not just once in teeny tiny text at the bottom of your website. Try in a bold headline font right at the top, again in the middle and once more at the bottom for impact. Spread it across your socials, create cover photos and update the About Me sections.

Hopefully you're connecting the dots here and we refer back to that pesky niching again because if you're going to be singing and shouting about all the things you do, a consistent theme threads it all together. Once you have a message that's as clear as day in your mind. Repeat. Repeat. Repeat.

We know repeating yourself might feel really unnatural, and this is again where fixed mindset and limiting beliefs may begin creeping in because you may think no one wants to hear it and it'll be boring. We hear you and understand that you might think that saying it just once will suffice, and like Vicky, the floodgates will open as soon as you put a message out there.

But honestly? It will probably be missed. You don't want to give any reason for your potential clients to miss out on what you have to say. You also don't want to give them any opportunity to become confused.

Finally, start embedding your amazing message in your potential clients' heads so they cannot possibly forget about you! Think about when you watch a TV programme that has adverts in between (skipping over the potential fact that you fast forward through them). Commonly you will see the very same advert in each commercial break, especially in the holiday seasons like at Christmas or summer time.

Now let's say there are four commercial breaks and the same advert shows again and again. Let's think about why. You know how it goes. The catchy music takes over and becomes embedded in your brain, and you find yourself singing or humming it over and over. We call that an earworm here in the UK. Arrrghhh, how annoying when you just want to get rid of the tune! But it is also a very clever marketing tactic, and it flipping works! It achieves its goal of ensuring you become aware of, and more importantly, will not forget the brand.

Here are some mind-blowing statistics for you. Your audience ideally needs to consume at least 7 hours of content from you, with 11 touch points, over 4 platforms, to feel that they are familiar enough with you, and primed enough to buy. This means your prospective buyer should be able to consume seven hours worth of content across videos, podcasts, articles, emails and see this across various platforms. It's a bit like going for dinner on a first date and then at the end of the meal, being proposed to. You barely know the person let alone feel ready to commit to spending the rest of your life with them!

This much content sounds a lot though, right? It actually may be easier than it initially sounds if you learn to work smarter, not harder. Repurposing content is a great way of saving time and avoids having to think of new ways to say things. A short video or live shared on your socials could have phrases extracted to produce a written post, blog, email, or e-book too.

Our podcast allows us to do exactly this, which is why it is not only a source of free valuable information, but a great marketing tool.

Helping your audience to know, like and trust you and your brand before you attempt to sell anything to them is an essential strategy, but one that can be overlooked. It is commonly the case that dog trainers become so immersed within their own businesses and focus solely on what they can do best for the dogs and what services would suit the dogs, that the clients can inadvertently get left behind.

Simplifying your messaging will go a long way to retain your customers' attention rather than overwhelming and repelling them.

Go all in on your purpose and weave in stories to tell people about how you deliver that purpose. Do not underestimate the power of storytelling and the importance of connecting with the humans you're wanting to help. You can invest in the best marketing agencies but without getting your messaging right, your content may still fall flat.

Chapter 9
Lead Generation

Getting more people to enquire with you is probably a thing you would like to know more of how to do successfully. You may have even dabbled with working on various strategies to get people enquiring with you to see which one you like and what works for you.

It was a common phrase we found ourselves thinking on more than a regular basis: "I just need more enquiries and then everything else will be fine."

Lead generation essentially means getting people into your world so that you have the opportunity to sell them something. It can be difficult to get right if there is a lack of strategy around whether or not the places you are targeting to obtain potential enquiries from is first, where your ideal client even hangs out, or second, if the type of messaging you're putting out is right for them or not.

Many people think they need more leads and enquiries fast, but without a good strategy around it, the method you choose to do this might end up not quite working as well as you might have hoped and this impacts your valuable time. One tactic that is commonly used across different industries is a post on social media where all the tangible aspects of the service or programme are talked about, like a package deal of five sessions, a training plan and Whatsapp support, all wrapped up with a discount. The whole post ends up looking like an advert which could be perceived negatively by potential customers because they're essentially being sold to and not being given reasons to connect with you. Fear not if this is you. This chapter will give you some ideas on how to do things differently.

There are two key concepts for generating leads: organic and paid. Paid lead generation is where you invest financially to get your business name and mission out to a wider audience through mediums such as Facebook ads, Google ads and any investment you make consistently on driving enquiries into your inbox. Organic lead generation is where you invest in building awareness of your business with very little financial investment. The one thing organic strategy does is drain your time investment in the short-medium term but hey, it's pretty much free!

Paid Lead Generation

You may have gone straight to a paid lead generation strategy thinking it'll be quicker and get better results. It almost promises to get your name out to a wider audience in a more professional way, so that all you have to do is sit back, watch the enquiries come flooding, and respond to them to your heart's content and while making lots of money.

We've already mentioned that Jo's background was in an advertising agency. Her role as Account Manager and Director over the years meant she had access to so many different teams that all made up marketing strategies. There was an artwork and creative team who she would ultimately give a written brief to (a fancy word document) containing what the client was trying to achieve within their marketing strategy. It was their job to turn that information into something pretty (a bit like when we don the marketing hat and put ourselves into Canva world). There was a copywriting team who were roped in when artwork needed copy to connect with its intended audience. There were website teams, social media managing departments, social media advert departments, a production department for when something needed to be printed. There were SEO departments to help websites, landing pages and adverts all work beautifully on Google. A whole host of top-notch skill sets were available at her fingertips for each of her clients budgets and aims. Whilst this was all amazing during her time in those positions, it actually served as a hindrance when she left and went on to create Paw Education dog training and behaviour in 2014.

Due to the knowledge she had about everything that could be and "should" be done, she launched straight into investing in paid lead generation strategies. She had around £10,000 available to her when she left that job and all of it disappeared in what felt like overnight in a company that built a fancy website, did the SEO implementation set up, created a Google advert and then helped her understand that she had to write blogs and do video blog content to support the SEO with templates they provided. Even though this had been her role for the previous 14 years, the overwhelm hit hard.

This was a completely different kettle of fish now it was her own business, and whilst £10,000 was a huge investment, it was an absolute waste of time and money in those early days because not only was there no clarity in what she was doing as the previous steps of this book hadn't been actioned, but when you invest in paid, you have to keep investing in paid. Yes, it worked in that it absolutely generated enquiries and sales were being made, but upon reflection those clients she was seeing in the early days were absolutely not who she wanted to be working with. She was also having to see double the amount of clients to turn a profit because the ad spend varied between £300 to £700 per month when she was only charging £30 to £50 per session. It took a lot to break even. At that time that thought didn't even enter her head because the paid-for machine was working. It was doing what it was supposed to be doing which was generating enquiries that she could sell to.

You can absolutely jump in with a paid strategy and it may get you results. The downside is that when your business becomes so reliant on paid strategies alone, anytime something goes wrong, or even just becomes different, with the ads, it has a big impact on your business' visibility. You may think this will never happen to you, but it absolutely could. An algorithm only needs to change a little bit and boom! Your advert stops reaching the people it originally used to. Or Google could undergo a huge update which means it will take a few weeks for everything to settle down again in the background, affecting your business in that interim period.

There are massive upsides to paid strategies when you have the overall strategy right and have crystal clear clarity in your messaging and offer. Advertising can hit straight at your exact target audience because of the data we all share about ourselves regularly with the likes of social media and Google. You can literally ask social media to find people who own dogs within a five-mile radius of your post code and continue to select various other traits including what you think your potential customers interests may include. Ads work really well when your service offer is right and you have a product or service that is a higher ticket price to make it worth your while. This is why for Jo it didn't work well as a long term strategy because her pricing and offer were never going to compete, unless she grew her team substantially to support the delivery. There are companies doing amazing things with paid ads that have endless opportunities because they allow you to reach so many more people and get their name in front of them. The investment doesn't always need to be really high but it is important that there is clarity in the messaging and you know exactly who it is you want to be speaking with. Otherwise a lot of money could be wasted if this part of the puzzle hasn't been looked at.

Organic Lead Generation

Organic lead generation is more of a long term strategy where your focus is on building connections, whether with people or local business. It can potentially feel slow in the beginning because we live in a world now where instant gratification is high in our expectations. We are used to things happening quickly, which is potentially why organic methods are easily skipped for being too hard and not worth the return on time investment. Organic, when invested in, will pay off in the long term because it's creating a solid foundational pillar of your business. A good majority of dog trainers are sole traders servicing local areas so you have an amazing opportunity to go all in on this.

You may be thinking, "But I've tried reaching out to local vets and no one wants me because I'm not ABTC accredited or Level 6, or whatever it is they're looking for," or "There are so many dog trainers in my area and the other trainers have the majority of available clients in the area," or even "I've tried adding my name to social media posts when they pop up asking for a dog trainer in the area and still no bites."

We'd be lying if we said we never had those thoughts either. In fact, those examples we laid out stemmed from actual conversations we had with local vet practices and some clients. However, what we failed to realise at the time is that those were limiting beliefs that were holding us back, because not every single vet will say that to you. There are trainers, behaviourists, walkers, groomers all over the globe who have some amazing relationships with vets. It's all about the time that gets put into developing relationships, something again we took for granted in those early days that it felt like it should have been an easy thing to do and it was a given that our services complemented one another. When you hit pause and think about your mission and vision, you align your service offering and have clarity on your business, conversations can become a lot easier. The relationships you have the potential to create within your local area are endless and you may end up with some unlikely connections that could work really well for you. Think outside the box and go all in on creating amazing relationships with local businesses. They don't have to be just dog-related either.

In the book *$100M Leads* by Alex Hormozi, there are four ways he talks about generating leads.

- **Warm outreach**

  This is reaching out to people you already know and who already know you.

- **Cold outreach**

  This is where lots of financial investment comes in because you're having to spend money to get yourself in front of people who don't know, like or trust you. This approach also costs a lot of time; just think about the amount of people you hang up on when they say they're calling from a company you've not reached out to before they contact you.

- **Content creation**

  This is sharing your thoughts, knowledge and personality through various mediums. Hormozi suggests to stick with one platform and do that really well before moving on to another.

- **Paid advertising**

    And finally, paid advertising such as through social media and Google adverts.

Hormozi has a whole book dedicated to these four strategies. The purpose of this chapter for you is to bring awareness about how it relates to your dog-training business and some ideas that could get you started. Implementing the above can be done in a variety of ways. We'll go into the ones that we really like so you can see which one you may want to try. A note here though just to say that we're merely scratching the surface with these suggestions but who knows? It may lead to another book on this topic alone because there's just so much to say on this area.

Email List

Firstly, if you do not have a list of people with email addresses and phone numbers that are already in your world, create one. Generating a list of people you can reach out to who already know you or have done business with you is always a first choice for us. Your email list is yours and nobody can take it away from you. You may have a following on social media that's in its high thousands, yet if you do not have their email addresses and you lose that account one day, all of those followers could be gone in an instant. Having an email list means you can still speak with them. You can also add a subscribe button to your website or socials to start bringing new people into your world as a way to learn what you're all about.

This is again where your messaging comes in because you can start to speak to your potential customers by letting them know more about you, the purpose of the business and how your product or service can help them solve a problem they're either having or want to prevent. On the other hand, you may have already built or started building a mailing list or newsletter. But do you actually do anything with it? Have months gone by with tonnes of tumbleweed drifting by? No communication whatsoever and then, out of the blue, an email appears in your client's inbox effectively saying, "BUY THIS NEW THING I HAVE NOW!" If this is you, you are absolutely not alone, and it can be very common.

There can be negative thinking around email because some think it's an ineffective way to speak to people in this day and age and that email is very spammy. It doesn't have to be. Try using emails to tell your audience stories.

Think of it a bit like how you use your social media platform to talk about your weekend and experiences and tie it back into examples of how this relates to a service you're offering. Jo will regularly talk about something with the kids and how it reminds her of something dogs would do and when you think about the behaviour a bit differently, you can see it from a different lens. Connect everything together and use your messaging to speak with people and resonate with them. Our top tip for this is pick one day and time each week and stick to it, hold yourself accountable and just start. Create a habit so you know the email needs to go out each week regardless of how long or short it is. If you are worrying about having enough content, we are pretty sure there is something that has happened to you in seven days prior that can be repurposed into a short story to share with your audience. Maybe it's related to dog training, maybe it isn't.

When the time is right, your list can be used to let them know that you have something they can buy from you and this shouldn't come as a shock to anyone because it's the whole purpose of having a business. If you do nothing else, we recommend implementing at least this, and combining it with content creation for your website and social media. It's another long game, but one that many successful businesses implement.

Lead Magnet

This is where your potential customers are drawn to you like a magnet because of something you're giving away. By giving your audience some free value, this increases the trust in your business and in you. You could create a PDF handout of some top tips to deal with recall when adolescence hits, or you could have a pre-recorded video on body language. As long as it connects with your target audience and aligns with your business mission, you can offer anything as a freebie in exchange for an email address and phone number. This is where you'd then add the email address onto your email list so you can start nurturing them and let them get to know you more via your email messaging.

Referrals

Once you've exhausted your current list, and we mean absolutely exhausted it by contacting everyone you know who has worked with you before, it's time to move on to introductions, referrals and conversations. This basically means speaking with people to gain referrals and collaborate with others. Ask your existing clients for a referral, and even those people who are ringing you with an enquiry such as "Who else do you know that might be a good fit for the service I'm offering?"

Collaboration is something we wholeheartedly believe in and encourage you to do too. We know it can be a vulnerable thing to do due to the fear of judgement and potentially from having a scarcity mindset in terms of thinking there may not be enough business for you all in your area. Collaboration is a great form of lead generation because there will be people out there who compliment your services, plus you may struggle to fulfil every single person and dogs needs in your local area by yourself, even if you live rurally! Work together and strike up some conversations. You never know where it could lead.

Cold Outreach

When it comes to cold outreach, it's unlikely you're going to pop yourself in a call centre and ring around a load of people who own dogs, or at least that's the vision we have in our minds when someone says cold outreach. A great example for this industry is the local dog show. Dog trainers often love the idea of attending local dog shows and village or school fetes to connect with the community and sell their services. In theory, it sounds like a great idea getting known in your local area by being surrounded by loads of dog owners who are your perfect client. However, it may not be enough to convert potential clients onto your training services when the idea for most dog owners attending these events is to more often than not to have a mooch about and participate in the fun dog shows.

A broader strategy is needed to really make these events work and potentially thinking about the purpose of you attending these events and what you're wanting to get out of it. Vicky speaks from experience on this topic, having dedicated numerous weekends to similar events historically in her business without any real significant interest or monetary gain off the back of any of them. Her attitude was one of criticism on the attendees' part. "How bloody stupid are people! If only they knew the benefits of enrolling in one of my puppy classes, more fool them for not bothering. They'll soon wish they had when they start having problems in a few months!" were her thoughts.

There was something quite significant missing from the way Vicky was thinking back then. She was quick to blame the ignorance of these dog owners, but how on earth were they supposed to know the benefits? Were they even attending the event for the purpose of wanting to sit and chat about their dogs' behaviour when it was potentially a day out for the family. Vicky hadn't considered this and she wasn't clear in her mind about how she was going to engage with people at the event aside from having a banner, some leaflets and some treats to sell. There was a disconnect in expectation and a lack of strategic planning.

Think about how you could approach these events a bit differently. What about a Q&A on reactivity? Or your top five recall tips at your stand at a specific time? Forget sitting back and waiting for people to come to you, walk amongst the crowds and speak to people instead! Caveat, be careful not to try and use this free advice as a means of trying to convince someone to buy from you, but to genuinely add value and be in service of the person in front of you. Go back to your values and have them guide you to the outcome. Yes, they may have a dog, and are attending a dog show, and yes they may be thinking about getting some training help, but they know nothing about you yet and what amazing outcome you could offer them.

What a great opportunity to start building the like, know and trust elements face-to-face.

These strategies of creating gradual awareness may not necessarily bring in the fast cash and are definitely part of a longer term game, but it will start to elevate you by helping you stand out and become memorable. Adding free and appropriate value as the expert in your field will begin the vital nurturing process, and takes you one step closer towards being at the forefront of your potential customers' mind.

Regardless of which approach you may want to try, adding a human element along the way by speaking with people using your actual voice and preferably not hiding it behind text format is a massive help. If you need to use technology, try voice notes or video messages so it softens you and makes you relatable. They are likely to be received more favourably than you might realise. Despite the fact someone may decide not to work with you, the simple act of communicating using a human touchpoint may elevate their customer experience and leave a lasting impression. Even if the service isn't right for them, it might be for someone else they know.

As you might have realised by now, lead generation is a huge topic with so many ways you can execute different ideas. Pick the one that feels right for you right now and test it out. Compare it to how you'd consider all the different variables when dog training and rule certain things out before you write off the approach you're trying. Some tweaks here and there will always deliver different results. As with everything, have some fun along the way and enjoy trying different things and speaking with people. Just like dogs, we're social animals, and this is the part we get to really play with and learn things about others which will have massive impacts on your business and your well-being.

Chapter 10
Sales

Sales is the bit that a good proportion of the human population rolls their eyes at. For many of us, it's that part that causes something deep within us to go, "I hate this bit." It shows up more in this industry than most because dog trainers typically hide behind an email or text message when talking to a prospective client and really have no confidence in their own value. You may have forms on your website to receive client information, which is great, but with no clear way of someone being able to speak with you should they want to. If this is the client's only option, it may alienate those who want a more personalised approach. Although all of the pillars are essential to successful business strategy, the selling part of your business is one of the most important to focus on. You could have implemented the best lead generation tactics, got your messaging down to a tee and have put so much time and energy into crafting the perfect offer for your audience, however, if we fluff up the sales, then it is all for nothing.

For this section, we're going to focus on the sales conversation itself. This is the part where someone has left you a voicemail, booked a call with you or sent you a message after finding you, and decided that they want to find out more about you, your services and pricing, if those aren't already visible.

Firstly, it's worth noting that 80% of any purchase is driven by emotions and the remaining 20% is driven by logic. This means that the price part is a really small percentage of the reason someone may decide to work with you or not. A lack of sales can induce fear that leads to a reactive response such as suddenly slashing prices in order to drum up interest. This is a reactive response, and not something recommended as a long term strategy because it could actually devalue the knowledge and skills you've worked so damn hard to gain. Adding extra value by giving a free session or two is a much wiser strategy because the money you receive remains the same, but the client receives even more for it. Win-win!

Money is a big factor in your business and can often be thought of as a dirty word. Talking about it openly helps everything become a little clearer and even makes getting profit feel easier because it removes the stigma behind it. As in any walk of life, there are different views surrounding what money means to the individual, and so there are many reasons behind why this is the case, some of which we delve into within this chapter.

In its basic sense, money allows the business to stay open and pay yourself a salary for the work you're doing so that you can pay other service providers for the services that you use from them; the cycle continues all day, every day. So why are we so ashamed to talk about money and work towards achieving lots of it in an ethical way? There are those people who look at money in a scarcity mindset; Jo and Vicky both grew up with and still have immediate family members in their lives that have specific beliefs on money.

Common phrases we were both used to hearing included:

"Never spend more than you have in your account. If you can't afford something, go without."

"You should be putting money away for a rainy day and pension pot for later in life."

"I can't believe you've spent that much money on that! What a waste!"

"If you've spent that much, what are you getting out of it?"

The last one is interesting because this is unlikely to be a question aimed at you, but more at whoever is asking the question. Essentially, we all have different money beliefs and it all comes down to an individual's view on what they deem is valuable to them, and if it is a fair exchange of money for a product or service.

We recently went on a cheeky business retreat to Spain and our hand luggage restrictions meant we had only a 100ml limit for liquids. Vicky wanted some hair mousse but the miniscule version at the airport cost £7.70. Simply put, her desire for the mousse wasn't comparable to the investment she would have to make. Fast forward a few hours, and when presented with a bill for pre-dinner drinks at the hotel that evening, each one equated to £7. We valued the nice cold glass of rose wine we were presented with, and perceived this to be an adequate exchange for our cash!

This is why assumptions you make as a business of an individual's perception of money can be detrimental, and actually end up losing you sales. The best results in our dog-training business happen when we pick up the phone and talk to our prospects. Omitting this step in the past meant that we sometimes ended up working with clients we didn't gel well with, dealt with problems that weren't in our area of expertise, and received a general lack of key information ahead of the training journey that created difficulties later on.

Here is our advice on how to structure a sales call that allows both humans the ability to connect easily and quickly. It focuses on the required objectives, and clearly frames its purpose and desired outcomes.

1. Greeting and Setting the Purpose of the Call

As this is the first time you're speaking with them properly, it's a good idea to set the tone of the call and remind them of what the purpose of the call is.

For example:

"The purpose of this call is to get a quick summary from you about what made you book the call today, and secondly, I want to understand if we're going to be a good fit for one another and see if we'd work well together as a team."

By positioning how you're going to structure the call, this already elevates your position of professionalism and allows the person to feel that they are in good hands. It also alleviates the potential for the call to lose track, and receiving irrelevant information about the dog.

2. Ask Questions to Understand More About Them

Once you have initial basic information about the dog and you're confident you'd be able to help, start asking your questions to understand the reason for reaching out.

"Thank you so much for sharing, that's really helpful to know. May I ask:

How long has this behaviour been happening for?

How does this behaviour make you feel?

What happens if the behaviour doesn't improve soon?

And how does that make you feel?

Who else is involved in your dog's life on a regular basis?

How does the behaviour make them feel?

Pop yourself into imagination world for a moment and let's assume you've enrolled on the programme with us; What does life with your dog look like now?

Describe to me your dream for when you bring your dog home."

Rephrasing a question with a how or who prefix particularly enables you to tap into the emotion behind the purchase decision and can provide a great deal of relevant information.

Any surface level answers to the questions you ask is the logical part of the purchase journey. This information is absolutely needed, but it is not the reason that someone will or won't buy from you. Focusing on the ideal outcome or leaning in on the problem that has driven that person to come to you in the first place is a much better way to help them understand the importance of them purchasing your service. If you look at how people end up in your world currently, they find you because you're a dog trainer and they need support with their dog. The hard part is done.

You may have found yourself leaning in on your strengths of dog knowledge and asking questions on sales calls such as, "What have you tried so far? What are you doing about it? How much time have you put into training the dog?"

All important questions, but they are not necessarily useful at this point. It may mean you now have more information and feel more confident about the situation and how you're going to handle it, but think about how that might leave the owner. They could feel judged, or unheard. If, in addition, you feel the need to start explaining a detailed pricing structure, the specifics of how you deliver your work, your accreditations, and past experiences with other dogs, in order to justify the price of the service, it could end up feeling unconnected and even starkly transactional. Your customer may also feel like you're talking about yourself too much and feel as though they're just being told a lot, but not actually being listened to.

Getting this bit right can impact your business positively in more ways than just the client connection. If you use words from conversations in your marketing and messaging, it can allow you to find out more about what dog owners are thinking and feeling, and it can also allow you to understand why someone may not go ahead with working with you on a call because you could ask them without making assumptions.

Questions your prospect really wants the answers to are:

"How is it going to help 'me' with 'my problem' specifically?"

"How is that valuable for me?"

"How will it achieve the outcome and results I want and need?"

"Do I relate and connect with you?"

"Do I feel heard and understood?"

"Do I feel judged?"

3. Dealing With Stalls

Ensuring the correct questions have been asked as in the sales call example above will severely reduce the amount of times someone uses a stall with you. A stall is essentially where a person tries to get out of making a decision there and then without just saying no thanks. You do this all the time! We all do. A few of the most common stalls include, "Sounds great, can you pop it on an email for me?", "I just need to speak with my partner." and "I'll have a little think and come back to you."

Whenever you hear these, we recommend thinking of it as simply feedback to know more needs to be done to delve further. Remember somebody making the decision to find help with their dog is emotionally driven, and the above stalls are what society has taught us we need to say to avoid a conversation of just saying "No, sorry." Sales and selling can feel really icky if you're leading with a money approach of needing some cash rather than looking at it from a place of genuinely trying to understand whether or not you and that person could work well together; and if you have the skill set and service to be able to offer a solution to their problem.

4. Agree on Next Steps

To finish the call off, avoid leaving the next steps up in the air. If they've used any of the above stalls, go back and find out more about the problem and lock in a time and date for the follow up call.

It is highly unlikely that they will call you back in a few days if the call ends in a blank. A more successful approach is to get another time and date locked in and set the expectations up for that future call. Lean in on the uncomfortable and aim to get comfortable in this space. It might be that their partner wasn't available on the initial call, or that a time consideration needs to be explored before a definitive decision can be made, and another discussion will be required to clarify, but aim to find out the real reason by the end of this call.

On the other hand, if it all goes well and they say yes to going ahead with you, we recommend taking the payment over the phone there and then, and definitely before you commence the service. This can avoid an awkward conversation about payment at a clients' house and having to chase an unpaid invoice unnecessarily. It also keeps momentum high by locking your client in and getting them officially onboarded with you.

Being professional in sales is about the whole process, even down to taking the money. Receiving an email with a homemade invoice asking for a bank transfer payment may instil seeds of doubt in someone's mind as to whether you are actually a legit business.

Get the professional edge by investing in a card payment software such as GoCardless or Stripe. There are so many available now that are quick, easy and make everyone feel protected.

In summary, by making the switch to having true two-way conversations, it can open up so many doors with regards to the way you run your business. It means that you know who you are going to be greeted by when you rock up at someone's house for the first time. You know the type of person they are and what their challenges are.

You can make a connection and have that similar first date experience where you are excited to meet one another again with a feeling of knowing them a bit better than being completely cold. They might welcome you into their homes more warmly instead of you feeling like you need to prove yourself.

Understanding and setting up your potential clients to succeed is essential for a good, long lasting relationship with them. The clearer we can be, the longer they are likely to stay with us. Taking the time to truly understand their struggles and desires in a way that is so personal and led with genuine integrity will enhance not only their but our entire experience along the journey.

Taking the time to get to know your clients inside out can make broaching trickier subjects, if and when they might be necessary, just that little bit easier. The type of language you use with one client may be different to the next, and you will only know that it won't offend or land awkwardly with them if you truly understand them. Spend time in the sales process going all in on trying to understand and lead with curiosity.

This is where the culmination of all the previous pages come together. Here is where we get to speak to someone about our genius, our passion, talk about the specially crafted service that will be the solution to their problem. Everything right from the start of this book leads to this part.

If you master your mindset, understand who you are, know your area of genius and have crafted an offer that is purposely designed for your target audience and understand your messaging, this bit becomes that little bit easier.

Conclusion

As we bring this book to a close, we want to extend our heartfelt thanks for embarking on this journey with us. We hope the insights, strategies and personal stories shared within these pages have provided you with a solid foundation for building not only a business you love, but also one that thrives. Being a dog trainer is an incredibly rewarding path, yet it comes with its unique challenges. It is our belief that you can create a business that not only supports your passion for dogs but also provides you with a fulfilling and happy life.

We've walked you through the core principles of our Business Basics framework. Each section of this book has been crafted with your unique journey in mind, focusing on the essential elements that will help you succeed both personally and professionally. Our aim has always been to give you the knowledge that, when implemented, will have huge positive impacts on your life and business. As comprehensive as this book may seem, it is important to acknowledge that the journey of creating a business you love is continuous. Learning and growing as a person and as a professional doesn't end with the final chapter of a book. We wish it could, yet as with anything in life that is worth having, it's a continuous adventure with lots of ups and downs along the way. We hope you can see how these strategies could improve the situation you're in now and give you clarity on what your next steps should be.

Reflect on the exercises and put them into practice, continually revisiting the concepts that resonate with you the most. Remember, the goal is to build a business that you love in its entirety, not just the dog elements.

We hope this book has also provided a sense of connection and community. You are not alone in this journey. Many have walked this path before you, and many will follow. Sharing your experiences, challenges and successes with fellow professionals can provide invaluable support and inspiration. Collaboration and mutual support are key to not only surviving but thriving.

As you move forward, keep in mind that building a business is as much about personal growth as it is about professional achievement. Stay curious, stay passionate and most importantly, stay true to yourself and your vision.

In closing, we want to remind you that this is just the beginning. There is so much more to explore, learn and achieve. Let this book be your guide, but don't stop here. Continue to seek out new knowledge, surround yourself with supportive and inspiring people, and never lose sight of why you started this journey in the first place. Your passion for dogs is a gift, and with the right mindset and strategies, you can build a business that amplifies that passion and allows you to live a life you love.

Scan the QR Code to get the podcast in your ears and take us along your journey!

Thank you for allowing us to be a part of your journey. We are excited to see where it takes you and are here to support you every step of the way.

References

[1] Mindset Works Team. "Dr. Dweck's research into growth mindset changed education forever," *Mindset Works*, 2017, https://www.mindsetworks.com/science/ (accessed 18 August 2024).

[2] Experian Newsroom. "Half of All New Businesses Fail Within Three Years of Opening," *Experian*, 2023, https://www.experianplc.com/newsroom/press-releases/2023/half-of-all-new-businesses-fail-within-three-years-of-opening.

[3] Mind Tools Team. "What Are Your Values?," *MindTools*, 2024, https://mindtools.com/a5eygum/what-are-your-values.

[4] Qualtrics Team. "50 examples of strong company core values", *Qualtrics*, 2023, https://www.qualtrics.com/blog/company-core-values.

[5] M. Keenan. "Mission to Accomplish: 17 Inspiring Mission Statement Examples", *Shopify*, 2024, https://www.shopify.com/uk/blog/mission-statement.

[6] LSA Global Team. "Aligned companies significantly outperform their peers," *LSA Global*, 2024, https://lsaglobal.com/insights/proprietary-methodology/lsa-3x-organizational-alignment-model.

[7] "22 vision statement examples to help you write your own," *Brex*, 2024, https://www.brex.com/journal/vision-statement-examples.

Testimonial

When you think about the business world, you might imagine boardrooms, high-stakes negotiations or tech startups disrupting industries. But there's a whole other side to business that's just as impactful, and often more fulfilling—the side where passion meets purpose. That's exactly where this book by Jo and Vicky comes in.

In an industry that's as dynamic and rewarding as dog training, success isn't just about knowing the right techniques; it's about building a business that's as strong and resilient as the dogs you train. Jo and Vicky have done just that. Their journey from passionate trainers to successful business owners is a testament to what happens when you blend expertise with an entrepreneurial spirit.

This book isn't just a guide; it's a blueprint for anyone looking to turn their love of dogs into a thriving business. Whether you're a seasoned trainer looking to scale up or someone dreaming of starting your own dog-training business, you'll find invaluable insights here. Jo and Vicky don't just teach you how to train dogs, they teach you how to build a brand, grow a loyal client base and navigate the challenges of running a business in an ever-evolving market.

What makes this book truly special is the authenticity and generosity of spirit that Jo and Vicky bring to their work. They understand that success in dog training (as in life) is about building trust, establishing clear communication and above all, nurturing relationships – whether they're with clients or canines.

After exploring the chapters within, you will be inspired, educated, and, most importantly, equipped with the tools you need to build your own successful dog-training business. Jo and Vicky have paved the way and now, they're handing you the roadmap.

Here's to building a business that's as joyful, loyal and tenacious as the dogs we love.

I am proud to call this dynamic duo my incredible clients and friends and can't wait to see their message and impact spread around the world!

Shari Teigman
Performance Coach and Creative Strategist
www.shariteigman.com

Printed in Great Britain
by Amazon